Victoria Ruvolo

Robert Goldman, J.D., Psy.D.

as told to LISA PULITZER

"No Room For Vengeance..."

IN JUSTICE AND HEALING

NO VENGEANCE PUBLISHING, INC.

NEW YORK

A Note on Sources:

This book is based on numerous interviews and dozens of news reports. We interviewed police, attorneys, witnesses, family members, doctors, medical staff and others tied to the story. There are no fictional or "composite characters" in this book, although at least one person has been given a pseudonym. Certain events, sequences, and conversations were reconstructed from a synthesis of all the evidence, including the confessions as reported in the media, interviews with participants and other information.

TABLE OF CONTENTS

INTRODUCTION

MY LIFE BEGAN TO CHANGE the day I started reading the newspaper articles about Victoria Ruvolo. Coming at a time filled with emotional turbulence for me, the unfolding of Victoria's story was at once horrific and inspirational; it was about the triumph of the human spirit. Even now, all these years later, she is still impacting my life, as she is the lives of so many others.

On November 12, 2004 forty-four-year-old Victoria Ruvolo was the victim of a reckless teenage prank that almost killed her. While driving home from her niece's concert on Long Island, New York, she was struck in the face by a frozen turkey hurled out of a passing car by a teenager. It was a profoundly stupid act and, frankly, the sort of stupidity that I have seen too many times in my career as a criminal defense attorney and practicing psychologist.

However, the story of what transpired in the weeks and months that followed that incident is what makes Victoria's journey unique and worth recounting today.

Victoria did what no one expected her to do.

Following the attack, she endured unbelievable pain and suffering, but she refused to simply seek revenge against the teen who had nearly killed her. Instead, she stunned the community and the Suffolk County District Attorney's office when she said she wanted to recommend leniency at the sentencing of Ryan Cushing, the young man who had thrown the turkey. She also wanted to find out more about him before she simply passed judgment on him out of anger.

When the incident took place, Ryan was still a teenager. But in the eyes of the law he was an adult and facing up to forty years in prison for what he'd done. Had it not been for Victoria's compassion for her attacker, he would most likely be sitting in prison for the next two decades. Instead, Victoria addressed the court and asked for leniency, giving him a second chance to have a productive life.

Like a rock tossed into the water that creates ever-expanding ripples, Victoria's act impacted many around her. Her act of compassion has had life-changing consequences for her friends and family, for Ryan and his family, and for people like me who hadn't known Vicky at the time but heard about her through media reports covering her story. The ripples from Victoria's kindness continue to affect how people react to adversity even today.

In choosing compassion and not revenge, Victoria demonstrated courage and refused to be consumed with self-pity. It would have been easy for someone who had been victimized the way she was to fall into a world of depression, helplessness, and remorse. But she rose above it all and became an example to others around her.

Today, Victoria and I work together to spread her message of hope and courage. With Vicky's help, support, and participation, I have created innovative new programs for use in schools, in the juvenile justice system, and other settings designed to keep kids like Ryan out of trouble.

We have all been victims at some point in our lives. When we are, we face two choices: getting dark and angry and retaliating against the individual or group we believe was responsible, or finding a more positive and responsible way to proceed. We are all connected; our actions have the potential to impact others, whether we intend them to do so or not. How we proceed depends on our awareness and our willingness to think through how our actions may impact others.

When we perceive ourselves as victims, we blame others. When we forgive, we have the courage to transcend the unfairness and move on. In fact, seeking vengeance has the potential to trigger a never-ending cycle of violence, whereas forgiveness often has the opposite effect, diluting the impact of the violence.

How we react will have a lasting impact on our own lives and upon those who are close to us. And, like a stone tossed upon a pond, our actions ripple across the lives of many others.

—*Robert Goldman J.D., Psy.D*

"He who seeks vengeance
must dig two graves:
one for his enemy
and one for himself."

- *Chinese proverb*

PROLOGUE

A LIGHT SNOW WAS FALLING as Victoria Ruvolo hurried into Macy's Department Store at Long Island's Smith Haven Mall. It was two days before Christmas 2009 and the aisles were jammed. She was trying to get to the perfume counter. She'd promised her brother-in-law, Jimmy, that she'd help him pick out a Christmas gift for her sister, Jo-Marie. He wanted to get his wife a bottle of perfume, but he wasn't sure which one to pick and Victoria had offered to help. She'd even promised to wrap the gift and drop it off to him in time for Christmas Eve.

Macy's main level was abuzz with activity. Dazzling arches of faux greenery entwined with thick red velvet ribbons created a canopy over the main aisle and stretched back toward the escalator, delicate clusters of the store's signature red stars dangling at their centers. The piped-in holiday music added to the joyful scene and had Victoria humming along as she slowly made her way through the throng of last-minute shoppers.

Despite the crowds and commotion, she felt good about being out and doing something as simple as holiday shopping. It had been nearly five years since the incident, and she thanked God every day for how far she'd come. Back in her early recovery, the noise and the crowds would have been too much for her. Even the simplest things had been difficult for her to manage.

There were a handful of shoppers ahead of her on line, so she took a spot at the perfume counter to wait her turn. It was fun for her just watching all the people rushing about. Unbuttoning her heavy winter coat, she allowed herself a minute to get lost in the frenetic scene.

Victoria had just asked the salesclerk for a bottle of Liz Claiborne's Soul perfume when she felt someone tapping her on the shoulder. She turned around to find a young man she didn't recognize. He was wearing a navy blue ski coat and was escorting a pretty, well-dressed woman on his arm.

"I know who you are," he said in a friendly, non-confrontational tone. "I'm glad you're doing well."

Victoria could feel her eyes tearing up, as they did every time someone approached her in this way. Her ordeal had once been front-page news and had been picked up by the local TV stations as well as the national media. Even Oprah's people had called her about appearing on her show. It had been hard for Victoria to understand the ongoing interest in her case and why people had been so moved by the compassion she had shown the teenage boy who had nearly killed her.

Now, here it was nearly five years later, and in the midst of the holiday shopping frenzy, she was being recognized once again for what she had done for her eighteen-year-old assailant that day in court.

"Thank you," she replied, crossing her hands over her heart to convey her appreciation to this nameless shopper. "I'm truly grateful for everyone's thoughts and prayers."

The man smiled. "Hats off to you! You did a wonderful thing," he said cheerfully.

"Merry Christmas."

CHAPTER ONE

"It is 10 p.m., do you know where your children are?"

Public Service Announcement

So often, momentous events in our lives happen when we least expect them. The assault on Victoria Ruvolo, which changed her life, my life, and the lives of so many others, started with a group of teens looking for a night of fun and a stolen credit card. This is a cautionary tale for parents who believe their own children are incapable of the kinds of mistakes that make headline news.

On November 12, 2004, Erica Karnes and her husband, Brad, arrived at the Island 16 movie theater in Holtsville, Long Island, pulling into the first available parking space. Karnes had recently given birth to the couple's third child, and this was her first night out with her husband since the baby had arrived. Karnes, a stay-at-home mom, was looking forward to the evening, but, as usual, she was running late.

Teasing her about her chronic tardiness, Erica's sister and brother-in-law had bought the tickets ahead of time. Brad already had them in his pocket as they pulled into the sprawling parking lot. Still, fearing they'd end up in the neck-craning seats in the front row, Erica parked the car, grabbed her coat from the back seat, and hurried with her husband into the movie theater.

In her haste, Erica had left the minivan unlocked. On the rear seat sat her purse, barely visible through the car's tinted windows. She had deliberately left it in the car, not wanting to forget it in the movie theater, but she had not meant to leave the doors unlocked.

At the same time, three local teenagers were combing the Island 16's parking lot looking for mischief. Pulling misdemeanor pranks had become a Friday night ritual for the group. One of the young men had already racked up a police record of criminal pranks. That past September, he had been charged with the unauthorized use of a vehicle after confessing to police that he and a group of friends had stolen a school bus and taken it on a wild, midnight ride. In a separate incident, the teen was charged with criminal mischief after he admitted smashing a minivan window while drunk with the intention of swiping the stereo equipment inside.

Predictably, movie theater parking lots are full of unattended cars whose owners will not be returning for at least a couple of hours. While the audience inside the Island 16 was admiring the lifelike animation of actor Tom Hanks in The Polar Express, the trio was walking in between the cars, looking for opportunity.

"Can you see anything?" one of them asked.

One of the three was getting impatient as the others pressed cupped hands against car window after car window, scanning the interiors for something to provide the evening's entertainment. The trio had been skulking around for nearly thirty minutes and the damp fall air was starting to bother them. One of them was about to suggest they go to a local diner and get something to eat when her friend, now peering into the rear seat of Erica Karnes's green Plymouth minivan, saw the purse.

The young man grabbed it without so much as triggering a car alarm as his cohort scrolled through the contacts on his cell phone.

Dialing friend after friend, he invited them to the Island 16 to join in the fun. A group of twelve teens soon gathered in a distant corner of the parking lot. In a convoy of four cars, they left the multiplex and headed to a nearby gas station to fill up their tanks.

"The gas is on Erica," they laughed.

After charging the gas for all four cars on the stolen credit card, the group went on its way, looking for stores that were still open. They came upon a Blockbuster, where they bought DVDs and popcorn. At the checkout counter, one of the young women in the group forged the signature because the stolen credit card belonged to a female.

"Hey, what about Waldbaum's? I think they're open twenty-four hours," one of them suggested next.

At the grocery store, a young woman was working Register #5, the only one open at 11:30 p.m. on a Friday night. To pass the time, she was thumbing through the latest issue of People when she heard laughter and looked up to see the teens entering the store.

They quickly dispersed, some grabbing shopping carts before dashing up and down the recently waxed floors.

"Hey where'd you get the shrimp?" one of them asked as he crunched on a cookie from a package he'd taken from the shelf.

"In the frozen section," his friend replied.

"Oh, there's a sale on turkeys," he laughed, checking out the freezers full of holiday birds.

"Come on, let's go, we are all waiting for you," one of the teens said.

"Okay, hold on, I'm getting a turkey."

Grabbing some stuffing, a turkey baster, and a roasting pan, the group headed to the checkout counter where the clerk had finished reading her magazine. The group laughed as one of the young men lifted a 20-pound frozen turkey from his shopping cart and placed it on the conveyor belt with the other items.

It was 12:25 a.m. and the store was practically empty. Most of the teens casually walked out, leaving two to assist the young woman who was using the credit card with the groceries. The packages didn't all fit in the trunk of the car, so one of the passengers loaded some of them next to him in the back seat. More were stashed on the floor by his feet. Finally, climbing into their respective cars, they took off. As they drove along Portion Road, the young man in the back seat with all groceries began to worry about getting caught.

He already had a criminal charge hanging over his head. He'd gotten in trouble for throwing eggs at his ex-girlfriend's house four months earlier and the judge in the case had ruled to dismiss the charges if he stayed out of trouble for six months. At the time, he'd been with a group of kids, but he had been the only one to get in trouble.

Now, here he was again, doing something he shouldn't be doing. What if they were picked up? He could get in serious trouble because he already had a case pending in criminal court.

He suddenly panicked. What if the car did actually get pulled over? How would it look to the cops finding him there in the backseat with all the packages, including the one with the frozen turkey, on his lap?

Even though it was raining, all the windows in the car were cracked open a few inches. Pressing the window control, the young man rolled his down the rest of the way and lifted up the frozen bird. Extending his arms into the sleeting night, he let it go. The music from the car radio was blasting as the car continued cruising along Portion Road.

Traveling on that same road that night was forty-four-year old Victoria Ruvolo. Her evening had begun at 6 p.m. when she pulled her red 2003 Hyundai into the carport of her snug, three-bedroom California-style ranch house in Lake Ronkonkoma and ran inside to get changed. Her friend Louis was meeting her in less than an hour and she wanted to be dressed and ready when he arrived. She was relieved that he'd agreed to accompany her to her niece's performance that night. Although it was not yet Thanksgiving, forecasters were already predicting snow showers for later in the evening.

Victoria hated to drive alone after dark, especially in bad weather.

Still, as long as she had someone in the car with her, she preferred to be behind the wheel and in control of the vehicle. Her fear was rooted in a sad reality. It had been snowing the night her brother Tommy had died in a car accident. Now, here it was almost twenty-seven years later, and still the idea of driving in the snow frightened her.

Five years prior to Tommy's accident, the Ruvolos had also lost Billy, the youngest of Victoria's three brothers, to an accidental drug overdose. With so much tragedy, family gatherings were especially important. As reluctant as she felt, Victoria was not the type to let her anxiety stop her from seeing her niece in her debut performance.

The show was set to begin at 8 p.m. at the Village Pub in Amityville, about twenty minutes away by car. Victoria wanted to be there in plenty of time to get a good seat. By 7 p.m., she was pacing through her living room, eager to get on the road. She didn't even give Louis a chance to ring the doorbell. As soon as she saw him coming up the driveway, she put her miniature pinscher, Gucci, into her kennel, pulled on her new Donna Karan coat and raced out the front door, locking it tightly behind her. While she knew most of her neighbors, Victoria was a woman living alone and she was diligent about her personal safety. She could hear Gucci inside the house, barking frantically and stirring up her two other dogs, as she hurried to her car and motioned for Louis to climb into the passenger seat.

Victoria and Louis were not romantically involved, just good friends. They'd been introduced through her former husband and had stayed in touch even after Victoria's marriage ended. Louis was some years younger and, through their friendship, he'd met and eventually married one of Vicky's nieces. But the marriage had soured and they were in the process of divorcing. Louis was upset over it, so he and Victoria had been spending a lot of time together commiserating about their failed romances.

Like Louis, Victoria was also nursing a broken heart. She'd recently split up with the man she thought would be her partner for the rest of her life. Even though she'd always thought of herself as an independent person, a part of her still felt like she needed a man to complete her.

She had been convinced that Ron, a mailman, was going to be that person. When things fell apart, she struggled to let go.

In an effort to move forward, Victoria had put herself on a strict diet and exercise regime, and she was ecstatic about the results. She had struggled with weight all her life, and at forty-four, she had lost 60 pounds and three dress sizes. For the first time, she was fitting into a Size 10. Still, without Ron she felt empty inside. She had a failed marriage, a newly fizzled romance, and the same job at the collection agency for the last seventeen years. In some ways, she thought her life had become stagnant.

Victoria arrived at the pub just after 7:30 p.m. Her sister, Jo-Marie, complimented her when she came in. She was especially envious of Vicky's well-tailored white jacket, a waist-length designer piece that Victoria had gotten on sale. Of Victoria's four sisters, Jo-Marie was closest to her. Just three years apart, they had shared a bedroom growing up on Sutter Avenue in Brooklyn.

A few minutes after 8:00 p.m., Victoria heard her niece being called to the stage. She watched in nervous anticipation as Jillian grabbed the microphone. She looked so grown up in her pretty white blouse and blue jeans, and Victoria's heart raced with excitement as the fourteen-year-old belted out the lyrics to Nirvana's Smells Like Teen Spirit. From the applause, Victoria could tell that the other people in the audience liked it as much as she did.

Victoria and Louis were having such a good time that she didn't realize how late it was. Her watch showed it was after eleven when she invited her sister to the parking lot to give her the toy she had bought for her dog, Mia. Like Vicky, Jo-Marie loved animals, probably because of all the stray dogs and cats her family had taken in growing up.

As she stepped out into the night air, Victoria saw that big wet flakes were beginning to mix in with the rain that was already falling and quickly opened her trunk to give her sister the present.

"I have to get going," she told Jo-Marie. She wanted to get on the road before the weather got much worse.

"Please stay a little longer," Jo-Marie pleaded. She didn't want the night to end.

"No," Vicky told her. "I'd better go."

Louis, sitting at the bar talking with friends, finished his drink when Vicky summoned him, and they went to the car. Since the weather was getting bad, she decided not to take the highways but use the local roads instead. That way, if conditions worsened, she could easily pull off the road without worrying about fast moving traffic.

The slower, safer route was without incident until the Hyundai was within a mile of home. By an unfortunate circumstance of timing, the slower route had put her car on a collision course no one could have foreseen. Though Victoria had exercised her utmost caution to get home safely, it would be impossible for anyone to protect himself from what happened next.

CHAPTER TWO

"It is better to take many injuries than to give one."

Ben Franklin

Victoria was just two blocks from her driveway when the windshield of her car suddenly imploded, sending bits and pieces of glass everywhere. Within seconds of the impact, Louis grabbed the bent and twisted steering wheel and frantically sought to keep the car under control. The unidentified object struck Vicky directly in the face, breaking numerous bones and leaving her barely conscious.

Almost immediately, Louis reached down in front of her and pulled her foot from the gas pedal. The wind and snow rushed through the broken windshield, and he strained to see where to steer the car to the side of the road. Unable to reach the brake pedal, Louis had no choice but to let the car roll to a stop. He steered toward an empty strip of shoulder and, tense seconds later, managed to stop the car without crashing into anything.

Struggling to remain calm, Louis cradled Vicky's head in his hands, a critically important move that kept her throat open and allowed her to breathe. In his younger years, Louis had been a volunteer for the Hauppauge Fire Department. His knowledge of first aid came flooding back as he sat in the passenger seat and focused his attention on Vicky, trying to keep her alive until police and ambulance crews arrived. Had he not been in the car, she would almost certainly have veered into oncoming traffic or careened off the road into a tree.

It is hard to imagine what it must have been like for Louis to see his friend in that condition. While she would suffer through the healing process, God spared Victoria the memory of the actual event. But Louis remained conscious and a witness to the horrific sight. In that moment he, too, became a victim of whoever had perpetrated this reckless act.

Time stood still as he carefully cradled Victoria's broken face and head in his hands so she wouldn't choke on her own blood. Within a few minutes help was on the scene, thanks to an unidentified passerby who dialed 911.

"Please help Vicky," Louis screamed out when he saw the pair of headlights slowing up beside him. He was still in the passenger seat when Fire Chief Jerry Curtin arrived from his home only one block away.

Like all firemen on Long Island, Chief Curtin was a volunteer. He was a member of the Farmingville Fire Department. During the day, he worked for the Suffolk County Morgue retrieving victims from crime and accident scenes. In that capacity, he'd seen his fair share of trauma over the years. Still, nothing could have prepared him for what he was about to encounter. As he neared the vehicle, the sound of gurgling blood alerted him to the driver's side of the car, where he saw what he would later describe as little more than a mound of flesh with shards of glass piercing through it. Victoria's face had literally been crushed from the impact of the partially frozen turkey, found later in the back seat by emergency personnel.

"She's having difficulty breathing," Chief Curtin shouted to his arriving team members. "Her airway is crushed."

There was no time to use the Jaws of Life, so Chief Curtin ordered a rapid extrication, an emergency rescue technique designed to move a patient from a sitting position to a supine position on a long backboard while maintaining stabilization and support for the head, neck, torso, and pelvis.

A hard collar was placed around Vicky's neck before she was swiftly strapped to a gurney and loaded into a waiting ambulance. Emergency workers used a knife to slice open her brand new Donna Karan jacket. The escaping feathers could be seen drifting in the wind and snow as the medics searched for a vein to start an IV.

Within sixteen minutes of the 911 call, Victoria was on her way to Stony Brook University Hospital, the closest to the scene and, thankfully, a Level 1 Trauma Center, the only one in New York's Suffolk County. Paramedics radioed ahead to alert the trauma unit that they were en route.

Dr. Mark Shapiro and a team of physicians, medical students, nurses and the hospital chaplain were scrubbed and staged in the emergency room when the ambulance crew rushed the gurney inside. Everyone was working quickly to get Victoria stabilized when one of the doctors asked, "How could a live turkey have flown through her windshield?"

He was trying to reconcile what he had heard from the accident scene with his observation that the blood covering Victoria's upper body was embedded with feathers. Other medical team members were wondering the same thing.

"Do you know your name?" Dr. Shapiro asked as he attempted to open Vicky's eyelids to shine a light into her pupils.

Remarkably, she managed to answer him amid gasps for air. "Victoria."

"Do you know what happened?"

This time, there was no answer.

Doctors would later explain that Victoria's face was so disfigured they had difficulty finding her mouth, but they had to work quickly in order to secure her airway, which appeared to be obstructed, given her intermittent gasps for breath. Her swollen tongue complicated the insertion of a breathing tube. Even after doctors successfully inserted it and connected her to a machine that would provide ventilation and oxygen to her lungs, she continued to struggle for breath. To complicate matters, she had also lost an enormous amount of blood.

A CAT scan and X-rays revealed that Victoria's trachea was damaged and air was leaking into the soft tissue surrounding her lungs. She'd also suffered numerous facial fractures and was bleeding into her brain. The most troubling aspect of her injuries was that her brain had swelled. Doctors feared it would continue to swell, putting her at risk of brain damage if they didn't put her in a medically-induced coma right away.

———————

Her daughter's debut a success and the party over, Victoria's sister Jo-Marie was comfortably in her bed and about to doze off when the telephone startled her. It was just after 1 a.m., and the bedroom was pitch black. Fumbling around, she found the receiver and whispered a sleepy, "Hello."

"There's been an accident," Louis blurted out. He'd been transported to the hospital in a separate ambulance and was in the ER still covered in blood when he placed the call. "Vicky's been hurt."

Jo-Marie was frantic. Her husband Jimmy wasn't home. They lived in Oceanside, the same South Shore town her family had moved to when she and Vicky were teens. Jimmy had agreed to work the late shift in order to be able to attend Jillian's performance that evening and was already on his way in to work when his wife reached him. He turned around, picked up his wife in the driveway, and the two drove directly to Stony Brook Hospital through the sleeting conditions.

"This can't be happening again," Jo-Marie cried out when she saw her baby sister's bandaged face. The grotesque sight instantly conjured up images of their brother Tommy, the casualty of the car accident years before. Victoria looked the way he had looked in the hours before his death.

In shock, Jo-Marie fainted, falling to the emergency room floor. She remained unconscious until an ER nurse revived her with smelling salts.

"Hasn't our family suffered enough?" she sobbed, as the nurse gently guided her and the others to the waiting area.

CHAPTER THREE

| "Crime is a wound that disrupts | the peace of the community." |

Denny Maloney, Community Justice Expert

November 13, 2004, was a busy night at Suffolk County's Sixth Precinct. Officers from the narcotics squad were out executing a search warrant on a house known for drug dealing, and detectives at the stationhouse were in a back room interrogating a suspect they'd picked up for felony assault.

Detectives James Brierton and Walter Clark were available to respond to the emergency call on Portion Road, and their sergeant dispatched them to the scene immediately. Before they left, they learned that a woman had been struck by a frozen turkey that had smashed into her moving car.

"Who would throw a turkey at a vehicle?" Detective Brierton asked his partner in disbelief during the short ride to the crime scene. On the way, they both pondered why someone would throw anything, let alone a turkey, at another vehicle. Their job was to make their best effort to catch the person or persons who were responsible.

Had it been an accident, had something on the road been propelled through the windshield, this would have been thought of as an incident that could have happened to anyone; indeed, many of us have been in a car that has been hit by an airborne rock spun off the road. The legendary filmmaker Alan Paluka was killed on the Long Island Expressway in 1998 when a seven-foot pipe in the road was launched into the air by a car in front of him and crashed through his windshield. This incident, however, was a criminal act, no matter if it was negligent or intended to cause harm.

This was not the first time that Detective Brierton had come to the aid of someone in grave danger of dying. On February 6, 1988, he had responded to a call in Port Jefferson. Julie Lyskell was out with friends and family at Pasta Pasta, a small but upscale restaurant on East Main Street in the historic village, celebrating her 48th birthday. Julie was looking at the dessert menu when she suddenly slumped onto her husband's shoulder. Initially, her husband thought that his wife might simply be exhausted, but her heart had stopped beating.

Brierton, a patrol officer at the time, responded to the 911 call within two minutes and restarted Lyskell's heart with a newly-purchased automatic external defibrillator, making her the first person in Suffolk County to be resuscitated by the life saving device. Since her near-death experience, Lyskell has made it her mission to educate people about sudden cardiac arrest and the importance of accessibility to automated external defibrillators at beaches, sporting events, in schools and in all police cars. There was a degree of prescience in that event.

The Sixth Precinct was only two miles from Portion Road, but it took Brierton and Clark fifteen minutes to make their way through the barricades, police vehicles, and fire trucks that lit the night. The two detectives were escorted to what was left of Vicky's red Hyundai. They were shocked when they saw the gaping hole the turkey had left in the vehicle's windshield and the damaged steering wheel that had thankfully taken some of the brunt before the frozen bird struck her in the face.

"How the hell could anyone survive this?" Brierton mused aloud, noting that the car's interior was bathed in blood.

Behind the passenger seat was the tattered turkey. Police and fire personnel were eager to see what had caused all the damage and crowded around the car as the detectives carefully lifted the twenty-pound bird into the light to get a better look.

Police had interviewed several people who claimed to have seen someone throw something from a passing vehicle, but they couldn't provide much description because the night's poor visibility had prevented them from observing other details. With little to go on, the detectives knew their chances of finding the perpetrator based on eyewitnesses were not favorable and that they would need to pursue other leads.

A closer examination of the turkey and piecing together the shreds of the plastic wrapper revealed that it was a Shady Brook Farms product. A small, white label affixed to the wrapper read "Waldbaum's, Portion Road."

It was approaching 2 a.m. when Brierton and Clark set off for that particular Waldbaum's. The store was open 24-hours, although at that hour, there didn't seem to be any shoppers. The young woman at checkout counter #5 was now flipping through the pages of the National Enquirer. She was a little taken aback when the officers approached her, flashed their badges, and began asking questions about the torn plastic cover they'd removed from the turkey.

"Can you tell us when this was purchased?" Detective Clark asked.

"I need to check the serial number," she said smiling nervously, taking the wrapper from the officer's hand.

The two men waited as she passed the label beneath the cash register's optical eye. The serial number was barely legible and no information came up. "I can't read it, but maybe it will work if I type the number in."

Brierton and Clark waited in silence, hoping they were not wasting their time.

"Here it is," the cashier suddenly exclaimed. "The turkey was purchased here at 12:20 a.m. with a MasterCard belonging to Erica Karnes. She was with a bunch of teens. I remember because I thought it was strange that they were buying shrimp, Christmas decorations, a turkey and other things that didn't seem to make sense. The total amount came to $170."

"Do you remember what they looked like?" Clark asked.

"Not really because there were a bunch of them running around the store and they left really quickly after they got everything."

By this time, the store manager had come over to see what was going on. "We have store video cameras that might have caught the individuals buying the turkey," he interjected, pointing to the bank of cameras directly overhead.

"Follow me," he then instructed, leading the two officers up a flight of stairs to an office, which overlooked all the cash registers in the store.

Brierton and Clark waited as the manager hit the rewind button on the large monitor. The recent image of the two detectives talking to the register attendant popped on the screen. As the tape continued to rewind, Detective Clark saw something useful.

"Stop there!" he shouted.

The manager hit the button to freeze the frame. On the screen was a picture of the cashier in her green Waldbaum's jacket and a customer. The customer was placing a turkey, a tinfoil pan, a bag of shrimp, and some Christmas decorations onto the conveyor belt of Register #5. The man was in his teens, Caucasian, of a thin build, with blond hair. He was wearing a white hooded sweatshirt. Standing next to him was a girl who also looked to be in her teens. She had black hair and was dressed in a black hooded sweatshirt. And there was a third teen with short black hair, a thick frame, and a striped dress-shirt standing at the end of the counter bagging the groceries.

As the officers jotted down some notes, Detective Brierton's phone rang. The hospital was calling with an update on Victoria's status. She was in critical condition and there was a good chance she wasn't going to survive. Both he and Clark wanted the surveillance videotapes before they were lost or taped over, but there was little time for them to obtain a search warrant.

"We need this tape," Brierton told the store manager.

"Anything we can do to help," the manager responded, handing them the tapes and the store receipt.

———————

Erica Karnes did not realize that someone had taken her pocketbook until the following morning, when she was leaving the house to attend a baby shower and couldn't find it. After searching the house and double-checking in the minivan, she logged onto the computer to see if her credit card had been used. She saw that $300 worth of merchandise had been charged to her card since late last night, including purchases at a Waldbaum's supermarket, two Blockbuster stores, and a gas station.

She was angry and upset at the personal violation and the theft of her property. Some of her son's favorite video games had been in her purse and now they were gone.

Hoping to learn more, Erica climbed into her minivan and drove to the Waldbaum's on Portion Road. There, she spoke to one of the checkout clerks. She was angry that the cashier who had checked the teens out the previous evening had not verified the credit card signature, and she sought out the store manager.

The manager explained that the police had been to the store and had told him that an item purchased with the credit card had been used to harm someone.

When the manager explained that the teens had purchased a frozen turkey and one of them had thrown it out a car window, critically injuring a driver, Erica was overcome with guilt. Not only was she embarrassed that she had failed to lock her car door, she now blamed herself for the woman being harmed. She met with police on the case and continued to follow the story closely in the news. The victim, it turned out, lived in her neighborhood.

Vicky's story was front-page news in the New York area and was being covered by all the major television news programs. Before the media even learned her name, fear was the immediate reaction. The *New York Post* headline blared: "HORRIFIED KIN ASK: WHAT IS THIS WORLD COMING TO?"

Fear is the emotion that keeps us alert and mobilizes us. It's a primal emotion, the one that caused cavemen to flee toward safety from a dangerous predator. When news of an innocent driver being struck by a tossed frozen turkey reached the public, it naturally created a great deal of fear.

At the time Victoria was injured, the daily newspaper, *Newsday*, ran a story about road debris with the headline of "Driver's Worst Nightmare," listing four recent deaths that were the consequence of unexpected objects hitting moving vehicles. Knowing whoever had done this was still at large, motorists feared for their safety on the roads.

In addition to fear, there were also understandable feelings of anger. As word of the incident spread, the community outcry began in earnest. People felt a need for justice, an act of retaliation against those who were involved in such a profoundly foolish prank. Those feelings could be intoxicating.

The *New York Post* captured the sentiment correctly in its headline "RAGE AT 'TURKEY PRANK' THAT PUT DRIVER IN COMA." This outrage was intensified not just by the seriousness of the injuries but also by the reported generosity and kindness of the victim. Newspapers detailed Victoria's compassion, describing her as a caring person who had even purchased a mobile home for her homeless brother.

Pressure on the detectives mounted as media coverage intensified and reporters started pressing for answers. With help from the crime lab team, members of the Sixth Precinct were able to grab still images from the videotape. Pictures in hand, the search for the teens moved into high gear. The grainy images were immediately distributed to a group of uniformed officers who began canvassing locations where teenagers might congregate. They showed the images to anyone they could find. They also went to the local high schools and showed the pictures to students, but no one recognized them. Any new arrestees were also shown the images, again without any luck.

The search for the identities of the teens seen on the video was already underway when Victoria was prepped for surgery. She had been in a medically-induced coma for five days.

The timing of the surgery was critical. Packs of ice were being used to contain the swelling in her face until the inflammation in her brain subsided. However, the bones in her face were at risk of fusing if the surgeons waited too long.

Dr. Prajoy Kadekade had already met with her family in the emergency room. Though he looked youthful, Dr. Kadekade had years of experience, with medical training at the University of California Medical School and residencies at the Irvine Medical Center in California and at New York Presbyterian Hospital in Manhattan.

The damage to Vicky's face was so severe that Dr. Kadekade had asked the family to provide him with pictures of her that he could use as a reference during surgery. He literally had to rebuild her facial bone structure.

Fluorescent lights illuminated the operating room, and the heart-monitor tracked her heartbeat. First, Dr. Kadekade removed the breathing tube from her mouth and inserted one directly into her trachea through an incision. He used a retractor to open her mouth and expose her teeth. To better redefine her facial structure, he wired her jaw shut. Vicky's jaw was then able to provide a foundation for the next steps.

The surgeon then made three incisions, two below each eyelid and one along her gum line. He began lifting the fleshy portion of Vicky's face to expose the broken bones beneath. Slowly and meticulously, he peeled the swollen skin tissue until he could see the fractures.

Using the 3D facial CAT scan as a reference, Dr. Kadekade placed the first L-shaped titanium plate in position between two broken bones. Once satisfied with its positioning, he took a tiny screwdriver and began screwing the plate into position. His work was delicate and painstaking. He had to proceed slowly and carefully. Hours passed as Dr. Kadekade did the same procedure with three remaining plates. After the plates were installed, he fixed Vicky's broken eye socket with a special wire mesh.

The surgery lasted more than ten hours.

———————

Detective Brierton had not taken off a shift since the investigation began. Five days had passed and still police had no viable leads. Finally, Officer Garcia, who was sitting nearby, took the all-important call.

"Sixth Precinct, Officer Garcia."

"I have some information that will be helpful about the lady who got hit with the turkey," the caller said, identifying himself as Jack Cutrone.

It was the break that Detective Brierton had been waiting for. Taking the line, he offered to pick Jack up at his landscaping job, but the teen assured him that he'd be there shortly. Fifteen minutes later, Cutrone walked through the door, and Brierton was at the front desk to greet him.

"You want a soda?" Detective Brierton asked.

"No, I'm O.K."

Brierton led him through the precinct to an empty office in the back of the bare-bones police building on Middle Country Road. Jack sat down at the table. The detective walked around to the other side and sat down across from him, pen and pad in hand.

"That night the lady got hit, I was the driver with my girlfriend, Rachel MacDonald, who was sitting in the passenger seat, and Ryan Cushing was in the back seat."

Ryan Cushing and Jack were childhood friends.

Did you know that Ryan was going to throw the turkey?" asked the detective.

"No," Jack said. "He told us he was going to cook it later." He then contradicted himself. "I told him he could seriously hurt somebody if he was going to throw it. He said something like, if I throw it at the door it won't hurt anybody. I told him if he was going to throw the turkey he was going to have some serious problems with me."

Cutrone continued: "A minute later, I felt my car rock a little. I looked in my side-view mirror and I could see Ryan was hanging out the back window. When I realized that he threw the turkey out the window and he hit someone, I pulled over in a parking lot and smacked him in the head. I should have gone to check on the lady, but I got back on the road. I was infuriated that he hit the lady, she didn't deserve it."

Detective Brierton knew he needed to find Ryan, the one who had actually thrown the turkey.

"Can you get take me to Ryan and Rachel?" he asked.

"Sure." Jack was not viewing himself as a defendant in the case. Instead, he thought of himself more as the detective's newly-deputized partner. Together, they climbed into Detective Brierton's car. Brierton knew he had to keep Cutrone talking to him, providing more incriminating evidence against the others who were involved.

"You want anything to eat Jack, pizza or McDonald's?" the detective asked.

"How about some pizza?" Jack responded.

As the two ate, Brierton charted their course. "I think we start at Rachel's house first," Brierton said. "Then, I'll need you to give me directions to Ryan's house."

With the plan in hand, Detective Brierton and Jack went to pick up Rachel MacDonald, who was expecting them. Jack had already called her to say that he and a detective were on the way. Jack also called Steven Manzolina, another of the teens, who agreed to turn himself in, as did his girlfriend, Amanda McDonald, no relation to Rachel.

Cutrone guided the detective along the secluded and private roads of the North Shore to Ryan's house. "I would never have found this house if it weren't for you," Brierton said appreciatively.

At times, kids assume that their friends will protect them, and maybe all of the teens in this case believed that this was the case. I have met many teens who appear shocked that their friends snitched on them. But loyalty ends when freedom is threatened. As Detective Brierton may have explained to Jack Cutrone, there is a term in criminal law called "acting in concert", which states that when you commit a crime with someone else, you are as guilty as that person. For example, even if you do not steal the credit card, but act as a lookout, you can be charged with theft.

This is a very sobering concept to explain to a client who believes in his innocence because he was "just there." This lesson in law may have prompted Jack Cutrone to deny any complicity in Ryan's actions and be as helpful as possible to Brierton. From a psychological perspective, the teens were all doing the activities together, engaging in what is commonly referred to as "group think" mentality. This leads to the presumption that when everyone joins in, there is no personal accountability. So Ryan and his friends may have thought.

As Jack and Brierton approached Ryan's house, the detective felt for his handcuffs in anticipation of an impending arrest. However, after they rang the doorbell three times without an answer, they knew no one was home.

———————————

In law school, I learned about the "thin skull plaintiff," also known as the "egg shell plaintiff." It stands for the concept that in a civil lawsuit, you "take the victim as you find him." The doctrine came from an 1891 case that involved a 14-year-old plaintiff who had been kicked in the leg by a 12-year-old child while playing. The kick resulted in a worsening of a previous injury that eventually led to permanent incapacitation of the leg. Although the child was unaware of the preexisting injury, the 12-year-old was still held responsible.

Courts have reasoned that the defendant is responsible for all consequences which follow in an unbroken sequence, without an intervening efficient cause from the original act, even though he could not have foreseen the particular results, which did, in fact, follow.

As a psychologist, I often question if our world would be a better place if we lived according to the "thin skull" principle. Perhaps if we acted under the belief that all of us are thinly skinned and interconnected, this awareness would make us more empathic towards each other.

Surely, the teens who stole the credit card were not thinking of the possibility of the catastrophic chain of events that ensued in a few short hours. Ryan probably figured that he had never done anything especially bad, that his actions were all harmless kid's stuff. Once, his friends had stolen some apples from a farm stand and chucked them out the car window so they could watch them break apart in the roadway. Another time, they'd driven through residential neighborhoods, picking up big bags of leaves, holding them outside the car window, and then throwing them and watching them explode on the pavement.

Truth was, Ryan and his friends still needed their parents to provide structure and boundaries. They needed to be steered away from risky behavior. The teens were not best served by engaging in inappropriate social activities to stave off boredom. It's unclear if these kids had a curfew, but if so, it wasn't being respected. Their parents had an obligation to make sure their children were accountable. Although the parents may have felt that their children were grown and able to take care of themselves, most of them were still minors under the law.

———————

Having learned that Ryan was being sought by the police, Ryan's family attorney, Vincent Trimarco, arranged for the teen to turn himself in to police that evening.

News of Ryan's surrender permeated the media as reporters and camera crews staked out the Sixth Precinct. To the flash of cameras and calls from reporters for comment, Ryan walked into the one-story building with his father and attorney around 6:30 p.m., where

Detective Brierton was in the lobby to meet them. Ryan's goodbye to his father was fleeting.

Slouching slightly, Ryan was escorted back to the detective squad room. There, he was led into an empty interrogation room and handcuffed to a chair. The teen's attorney, Vincent Trimarco, had already advised Detective Brierton that he was not to question Ryan, so there wasn't much he could ask beyond Ryan's name, date of birth, and legal address.

"Any other names you go by?"

Ryan had no nickname, but he quickly created one. "Champ," he said.

It proved to be another foolish, immature move. The nickname would be used against him when the media got wind of it, portraying the kid as a cold, heartless criminal who considered himself a champion.

———

Once the fingerprinting was completed, Ryan was led down a corridor to a row of three cells. In the first cell, he saw Jack, asleep and quite content. Steven was in the second cell, and the third was reserved for Ryan.

At three in the morning, Brierton woke up the three detainees so they could be transported to Suffolk's Criminal Court building in Central Islip, where they would be arraigned. Because of the media attention the case was drawing, the detective knew that the teens would be given a "perp walk," paraded in front of the media so that newspaper photographers and cameramen from the local TV outlets could capture their pictures and shoot some tape.

As they left the precinct building, the three young men were shackled together. Police gave Ryan the choice spot right out in front. He was followed by Jack, then Steve. Cutrone's girlfriend, Rachel MacDonald, was walked out separately to the waiting police van.

Ryan was silent during the half-hour trip from Selden to Central Islip. Perhaps because of his cooperation with authorities, Jack did not appear at all concerned about the pending arraignment as he sat handcuffed in the back of the police van.

At the arraignment, Ryan was charged with assault, reckless endangerment, and possession of stolen property. Jack Cutrone, 18, Steven Manzolina, 17, and Amanda McDonald, 17, were charged with criminal possession of stolen property. Rachel MacDonald, 17, was charged with two counts of forgery. Michael Hasbrouck, 18, was later charged with criminal possession of stolen property.

All of the teens were able to make bail, except for Ryan, who was remanded to the Suffolk County Jail in Riverhead and held on $250,000 cash bail. At the request of his attorney, he was placed on suicide watch. He was eventually able to make bail, spending two days in 23-hour lockdown before being released to his family.

CHAPTER FOUR

"Be glad of life because it gives you the chance to love and to work and to play and to look up at the stars."

Henry Van Dyke, author, educator and clergyman

I heard the story about Victoria Ruvolo and the turkey on the car radio as I was taking my lunch break and making my daily trek to visit my mother at my childhood home in Oakdale, Long Island. My parents, Mitchell, a medical doctor, and Carole Goldman, lived about twenty minutes from my job at the Suffolk County Department of Probation where I worked as the clinical psychologist for the juvenile population. I was a recent hire.

After receiving my doctorate in psychology from Hofstra University in 2004, I sought to broaden my professional work by seeking to combine the practice of law and psychology. Although I was a successful lawyer, I had begun to question my purpose as I watched many of my clients change status, going from being juvenile delinquents to being adult criminal defendants. Nationally, incarcerated youths have a shocking eighty-five-percent recidivism rate. Although good for business, it was not the best for conscience. I longed to find a way to intervene at an earlier point in time.

My mother had always been my biggest fan. She'd often come to court to watch me try my cases. She had great intuition. "Robbie," she would say, "That juror in the front row does not believe your client."

She thought I was better suited to be a psychologist.

Like her, I had a passion for helping people. Growing up, my mother taught my two brothers and me the importance of helping others who were less fortunate than us. At holiday time, she often invited people with no place to go share a meal at our home. She orchestrated birthday parties for geriatric hospital patients, enlisting me to serve as her photographer. She developed programs for alcoholics and invited me to sit in on the meetings. She also visited with cancer patients. But she didn't invite me to those meetings. Perhaps she thought it would be too painful.

It had been close to two years since her diagnosis of ovarian cancer, the silent killer. Ironically, my eldest brother and my father were both doctors and partners in an obstetrics and gynecology practice.

When my mother was first diagnosed, I pored over medical journals in hopes of finding a cure. With a feeling of overwhelming helplessness, I learned that her days were numbered. Her illness was following the course doctors and medical journals had predicted.

Turning onto Idle Hour Boulevard, my stomach began to sink. I was hoping my mom had been able to sleep. I was convinced that if she could get proper rest, her strength would miraculously return.

My parents' house was visible from the street and I was relieved to see that there were no ambulances in the long and winding driveway. Their house had once served as the greenhouse for the country estate of William K. Vanderbilt, a grandson of railroad tycoon Commodore Cornelius Vanderbilt. Years earlier, the greenhouse had been converted into a residence, but its one-of-a-kind glass conservatory remained intact.

I loved growing up in that house. As a kid, I could play hide-and-seek and never be found. On summer weekends, I'd hop up on my father's lap as he drove a tractor to mow the acres of green grass.

I half expected to find my mother in the kitchen that day, as she so often was. The room was quiet, but I could feel her presence nearby. In addition to caring for people, she loved interior decorating. When she was healthy, she'd hired an artist to paint a mural of birds, rabbits, and flowers that now covered the kitchen walls. She was too sick to climb the stairs to her second floor bedroom, so my father had set up a room for her in our den, where she now sat in a green recliner that converted into a bed at night or anytime she felt the urge to close her eyes.

"How are you, Ma?" I was happy to see her sitting up and trying to swallow a cracker with a few sips of Ensure, a protein drink to help her keep up her weight. Placing my hand over hers, I kissed her forehead.

"I'm okay," she said unconvincingly.

My mother looked frail. She'd lost her hair from the chemotherapy treatments, but bits of it were growing back. She'd always cared about her appearance and was always well dressed and manicured. But she was now becoming too weak to wear anything but her pink nightgown.

"You want anything to eat?" she asked, closing her eyes. Despite the fact that she could barely keep anything down, she was worried about me. When my mother was healthy, I would often call her and invite myself over for lunch. We spent our time discussing my criminal cases and life.

"We have some chicken soup that Filomena made," she told me, referring to the woman who had been hired as our housekeeper, but who had become an important and much-loved member of the family. My mother was too sick to cook anything, but she had taught Filomena all of our family's favorite recipes. It was almost as if my mother was still cooking for us.

I was frustrated to see that my mother was getting caught up in pessimism. The doctors had lost hope and believed it was just a matter of time. Giving up was not part of my mother's nature, or mine. She had shared with me that when she was a teenager, her mother had told her that she was not college material. She had never fully accepted that, and so, at the age of fifty-five, she had enrolled at nearby Dowling College and graduated summa cum laude with a Bachelor of Arts degree.

Now, sitting by her bedside, I was finding it very difficult to watch her accept her fate. The two of us were helpless and silently accepted the words of the doctors.

"Did you walk today?" I asked.

"Not yet," she whispered.

"Come on, Mom, let's get up," I urged.

The special mechanized chair raised her to a standing position with the push of a button. "Walk with me," she directed.

The walk these days was around the circumference of the dining room table. She hunched over the walker as she made her way. The wood table was carved and rectangular in shape, with ornate cushioned chairs surrounding it. As my mother slowly shuffled around the table, I remembered all the parties she had thrown and all the people she had entertained. The company had been diverse and the food was legendary. Now, my mother and I walked in silence, save for the sounds of her shallow breathing and the rolling of the wheels of her walker.

"Mom, I want you to come to our house for Thanksgiving this year," I insisted.

"I am too weak," she replied in a soft voice.

I was sad and angry. Thanksgiving was her favorite holiday. My grandfather had had a live poultry business in Harlem and one year he brought home a live turkey the week before Thanksgiving. Memories like that that still gave my parents' house such life, even during somber times like these.

"So how is your new job?" she asked. It was hard for her to speak in long sentences. All her energy was now being consumed by her walking.

"It's good Mom, I like it. I really feel I can make a difference."

"I have to sit down," my mother said with a gasp.

I noticed that our walks were getting shorter, as were our conversations. Guiding her back into the chair, I disappeared into the kitchen. I found my father sitting alone at the white Formica® island, the one that my mother had wanted to have replaced with a granite top. For whatever reason, money, or maybe he just preferred the Formica® to granite, my father had asked her to wait until the results of her upcoming blood test came back.

He knew the test results would carry bad news. Why couldn't he just give in to my mother's wishes? Did it make that much difference? "I don't think she is going to make it much longer," he informed me.

The prognosis from the doctors was dismal, and my father, a doctor, kept telegraphing the same negative messages as her oncologists. Why couldn't my father's attitude have been different? Why couldn't he have struck some kind of different tone? But it was not to be, and I hated it.

My father's experience had made him unnervingly realistic. In his years as a medical doctor, the majority of his patients with ovarian cancer had succumbed to the illness. But this was my first experience with this fatal disease. And it was my mother.

My parents had been married for more than forty years, and my mother could always pick up on my father's negativity. She didn't need to wait to hear the results of her blood tests; she just looked at his face. It was the same vibe the young group of doctors gave her when they visited her while making teaching rounds at the hospital. I wanted to surround my mother with hope and positive thinking, no matter how far removed from reality my overly optimistic projections might be.

I didn't want to listen to my father's somber diagnosis, so I picked up the *Newsday* on the island next to him. I read the sports section first and eventually made my way to the front page. "Hey, did you hear about this woman who was hit with a turkey while driving her car?" I asked, glancing at the story.

"It's all over the news," my father replied. "The woman probably won't survive and if she does, she will probably be a vegetable," he said, blending what he'd read in the paper with his own medical expertise.

"You remember, a similar thing happened to your mother and me fifteen years ago. I was driving when some kids threw a cement block over the overpass and just missed our windshield and hit the hood. It would have killed us. Stupid kids.

"I know they caught the kids because I received a check for the damages. I think the judge had them do community service, a slap on the wrist. I know that another person in someone else's car was seriously injured because he wound up in the emergency room at Southside Hospital. To this day, I get nervous every time I drive under the overpass."

"That's right, I remember," I replied.

Taking the newspaper with me, I went back to sit with my mother. She was in and out of sleep as the television played in the background. She had little patience, or desire, to watch anything. Filomena was sitting beside her and holding her hand when I came into the room.

"Did you eat anything?" my mother asked.

Filomena left so that we could speak privately.

"Yes, I had some soup." I lied. I hadn't eaten a thing. Seeing Dad in the kitchen had made me scared all over again and my stomach was in knots. My mom meant everything to me, and I couldn't face the possibility of her not being there.

"Hey Mom, did you hear about the woman who got hit with the turkey?" I asked.

"Yeah, I am glad they caught the kids who did it. I saw the pictures of them on television. They look like real losers, and they need to pay dearly for what they did," she responded.

This was not the answer I expected from my mother. She seemed bitter. I asked myself if this was the same woman who always wanted to help people, even become a social worker. Maybe this was the cancer talking?

"It says here in the paper that the victim was a very caring woman," I said. "She likes to take in stray pets and care for them. She bought a mobile home for her brother who was homeless. She has a heart of gold."

"So what did she to do to deserve this?" my mother asked. "They may have ruined her life. These kids need to pay. I hope you don't wind up representing them."

My mother was not alone in her sentiment. A lot of people shared her views. But I had spent years representing juvenile offenders, so I had a different opinion.

As a law guardian representing children, I had seen kids making stupid choices that resulted in near tragedies. I once represented a teenager who, with a group of kids, had smashed his neighbors' mailboxes. One of the mailboxes had crashed through a window, barely missing a sleeping infant. My client was a follower in the group, but he was still responsible for the reckless act.

In this case, the newspapers had featured photos of the teen suspects in handcuffs being led out of the precinct house during their perp walk. Each photo showed the kids with menacing stares.

The *Daily News* called Ryan a "Fowlish Fiend." In the photo accompanying the story, he appeared to be laughing in police custody. Suffolk County District Attorney Thomas Spota was quoted as saying, "These kids will be prosecuted to the maximum extent of the law."

I found myself studying the photograph in the newspaper when my mother's soft voice snapped me back to our visit. "Rob," she began, "why did this have to happen to me? I am a good person. I have always tried to be good to other people."

This was not the first time my mother had asked me this question. Like the other times, I had no answer. I realized that she was becoming angrier and less hopeful each day. She was turning into a vindictive woman who at times I could barely recognize. She seemed to want someone to blame.

Just then, Filomena called to me from the kitchen. My mother's heavy eyelids told me she was relieved that the housekeeper was summoning me. "Go along," she encouraged. However, I was not ready to leave.

"Listen Mom, Thanksgiving is next week and I want you to be there."

"Rob, we'll see," she said, her voice weak and tired. "If I'm going to start getting new chemotherapy, I cannot be around kids who may have colds because I will not be able to take the therapy."

Filomena and my father were outside bringing in the groceries when the telephone began to ring. Embracing my mother in my arms and wiping her tears, I was not up to answering it, so I let the answering machine pick up the call.

"Hi," my mother's voice could be heard on the machine. "We are not home right now, but in the meantime, be glad of life because it gives you the chance to love and to work and to play and to look up at the stars," she said in the message, recorded when she was healthy.

It had been a long time indeed since my mother expressed that positive outlook.

CHAPTER FIVE

"The injury we do and the one we suffer are not weighed in the same scales."

Aesop

Victoria was finally wheeled to a recovery room at Stony Brook Hospital following her surgery. Her family sat patiently by her bedside, praying that she would survive her injuries. Victoria's doctors were guarded in their comments, and it was clear they remained concerned about her survival.

Family members felt a sense of despair and helplessness. All they could do was wait. Some of them wondered why anyone would do such a thing to a woman who had never hurt anyone, not unlike my mother's question about her illness. Vicky's family might find comfort if there was an explanation.

Sometimes people are inclined to think that the one and only victim in a crime or accident is the primary person injured, in this case, Victoria Ruvolo. But the incident's impacts were far broader. There was Vicky's friend and passenger on that fateful night, Louis Erali, who suddenly had to fight to control the car, stop it by the side of the road, and then tend to his severely injured friend. Louis will probably never forget how his friend appeared that night as her gasps for air were mixed with the gurgling noise of her blood.

Victoria's sisters spent nights away from their own families waiting by her side. Victoria's niece, Jillian, blamed herself for the incident. If she hadn't been singing that night, if she hadn't invited Vicky, the turkey would never have gone through her windshield.

Erica Karnes, the woman whose purse was stolen, had done nothing wrong, but she felt responsible. People often feel guilty even when there is no logical or legitimate reason to feel that way.

In the weeks and months after the accident, Erica frequently asked herself what would have been different if she had remembered to lock her car door that night. If only she'd locked the door, the kids would never have gotten her credit card, or gone to the supermarket to purchase the frozen turkey. If only she'd locked the door, the turkey would probably never have been thrown. The truth probably was that these teens would have found another victim. But "what ifs" can become paralyzing, as Erica Karnes can attest.

————————

When Detective Brierton walked into the hospital room to update the family about the teens' arrests, none of Vicky's family members was even aware that there had been a break in the case. They were still by her bedside, waiting for some sign of hope after the ten-hour surgery.

Jo-Marie and Rita rushed to meet the detective in the doorway. They threw him questions in desperation, each competing to get hers answered first.

"Who were these kids?" Jo-Marie asked.

"Why Vicky?" Rita jumped in.

"Was this a college prank?"

"Did they know Vicky?" interjected Jo-Marie.

"Was this intentional?" countered Rita.

The detective waited quietly for a moment before attempting

to respond. He described his evening with Jack Cutrone and the arraignments that followed.

"It seems to be a stupid prank," he concluded.

———————

Across Long Island, outrage over the incident was growing. The timing was particularly disturbing, coming just two weeks before Thanksgiving and at a time when people were starting to concentrate on family and the upcoming holidays. The bizarre nature of the incident also created outrage. Why would someone intentionally throw a frozen turkey out of a car at night in such a way that it struck another vehicle? The anger grew as people learned that the teens had left Victoria to die on the side of the road that night; no one had lifted a hand to help her. How could anyone do that?

What would have happened if Ryan and his friends had not left the scene, or if they'd all turned themselves in at the precinct as soon as they heard that they had seriously injured someone? The public outcry would probably not have been as fierce, mitigated by the perpetrators having taken responsibility, shown remorse. But that had not been the case.

There were plenty of people who wanted to visit Victoria, among them 100 of her co-workers at the large collection agency on Long Island where she worked. But her sisters would only permit members of the family to visit.

Victoria's family watched over her tirelessly. Her brother-in-law Ben, the husband of Rita, stayed with her at the hospital day and night. Ben was some twenty-four years older than Vicky, and he sometimes treated her more like a daughter than a sister-in-law. Ben brought a radio into the room, using it to softly play doo-wop hits from the 50's. Another brother-in-law, Jimmy, Jo-Marie's husband, also spent countless hours at her bedside, driving straight to the hospital after work to care for her. Jimmy was working third shift at his job, but he still made time to care for his sister-in-law.

Victoria's sisters, Rita and Jo-Marie, also took turns going back and forth to the hospital, where they would often sit and cry for hours. With her mouth wired shut, Vicky drifted in and out of consciousness.

Vicky's relatives worried that hospital staff might give her only the most perfunctory level of care. After all, none of them knew her; she was just a comatose patient lying in a hospital bed. It's hard to care about an individual without knowing at least a little something about them. So, they created a colorful sign and hung it on the wall across from her bed. On it, they described what Vicky meant to them, and how special she was to her family.

As staff came through the room on their rounds, many read the tender, grateful sign:

Thank you for taking care of our very special Aunt Vicky. Though she has no children of her own, she has been a mother to all of us. She has cheered for our success and wept at our sorrow. She has cradled us as babies in her arms, held our hands as toddlers, and walked beside us as adults. She cares for her family, selflessly giving her time, energy, spirit, and love. She is always willing to lend a hand and has painted the nurseries of many of her great nieces and nephews. She is the life of the party and yet the best shoulder to cry on. She is wise and warm and full of life. And she has never said "No" to any of us. Beautiful in body and heart, and strong. She has been there for her family and has helped out of love. She is everyone's favorite aunt and asks for nothing in return. She is loved. Very, very loved. From the littlest baby to her oldest niece, everybody loves Aunt Vicky. So please continue to take care of her and remember how special she is to all of us. We only have one Aunt Vicky and we want her well again!! Thank you!

Francine, Jeff, Brianna and Julianna Greenberg

Several of Vicky's friends had volunteered to care for her adopted dogs and cats, showing up two and three times a day to feed and walk them. There was Gucci, the miniature pincher she'd rescued, and the formerly homeless cats, Mittens, Trouble, Poncho, and Muffin.

"How will Vicky ever be able to care for these pets?" Rita asked Jo-Marie one day. The sisters wondered, too, if Victoria would ever be able to care for herself. The surgery had been very difficult.

Despite the odds, Victoria was making an extraordinary comeback. Five days had passed, and she was no longer in danger of dying and, indeed, had started torturing hospital staff, although she still can't remember anything from this time.

Vicky's friends and relatives said that she'd often get out of bed and run down the hospital's hallway, heading for the elevators wearing nothing but her hospital gown. The nurses would always catch her before she got any distance from her room. Victoria just wanted to get out of the hospital, no matter what her condition.

One nurse told her sisters not to worry. "I'll keep her here," she said. She was a large woman and would lie across Victoria's body to keep her down if she thought it was necessary. Unfortunately for the nurse, Vicky had been doing a lot of exercise at the gym in Farmingville before the incident, and there were times when she would literally lift the nurse and herself off the bed. The staff had to resort to tying Vicky to the bed, so determined she was to leave.

Nineteen days would pass before she finally learned what had happened to her.

Once Vicky had recovered enough to be discharged from the hospital, her doctors agreed to move her to St. Charles Rehabilitation Center in Port Jefferson, approximately five miles away. Because of her traumatic brain injury, she had difficulty with her short-term memory and had literally no recollection of her stay at Stony Brook.

It was 3 a.m. on the night of December 12, 2004, when Victoria awoke in her bed at St. Charles, feeling groggy and disoriented. Vicky could hear the sound of muffled voices coming from the hallway outside the room, and she recognized the disagreeable, antiseptic smell that lingered in the air. The faint light coming in through the partially-opened door enabled her to see that she was in a hospital room.

"Oh my God, who's been hurt?" she gasped, struggling to sit up in the bed.

Victoria didn't think much of the pain she felt when she tried to raise her head from the pillow. Instead, she worried that someone in her family was hurt. She'd lost so many loved ones over the years that it didn't seem unusual to be in a hospital waiting for word on someone else's condition. She just hoped that this time it wasn't one of her sisters who'd been injured.

Although it wasn't easy, she managed to drag herself from the bed and shuffle to the bathroom to wash up. She tried to hurry and find out what was going on. She didn't remember how she'd gotten to the hospital room, but she was certain that someone had sent her to lie down for a bit while waiting on news. That was the way it had always happened in the past.

Bending over the sink, she turned on the faucet and splashed some cold water on her cheeks. The sensation of the water touching her skin was painful, but she was too sleepy to think much about it. It wasn't until she took a quick look in the mirror that she realized she was the patient. The face staring back at her was pale and drawn. More frightening still, she had a tracheotomy tube attached to her neck.

"Oh my God," she thought, taking in the image. "It's me. I'm the one who has been hurt!"

CHAPTER SIX

"God places the heaviest burden on those who can carry its weight."

Reginald Howard "Reggie" White, professional football player

Victoria was the youngest of her parents' seven children, but she was also the strongest. Even as a little girl, she had the emotional fortitude to cope with stress, grief, and most of all, loss.

Her mother, Josephine, was forty years old when Victoria was born on March 12, 1960. From the moment Victoria arrived she was "Daddy's little girl." Exactly twenty years separated her from her eldest sister, Jeanne.

Her mother always told her she was special because she was born en caul, with a shiny veil covering her head. En caul is a term used when a child is born with the amniotic sac intact around its head. These deliveries are rare, occurring in about one in one thousand births. It was thought to be a sign of psychic abilities, good luck, or a special destiny. Some in the psychic community believe that children born en caul have "different eyes", an ability in perception and thought that is extraordinarily acute.

Victoria's mother told her that in the Italian community, it was customary to save the caul, and the nurses at the hospital urged her to do so. But her parents chose to leave it behind when they brought her home from the hospital.

Vicky grew up in Brooklyn on the borderline of Richmond Hill and East New York. It was a nice neighborhood, although a little rough if you walked too far in any direction. She lived in a house that her maternal grandparents had given to her parents as a wedding gift, a brick semi-detached house on Sutter Avenue.

The neighborhood was well-serviced, with a drugstore, a pizzeria, a florist and a gas station on the block. Vicky shopped at the corner delicatessen whenever her mother needed something.

The Ruvolos' house was a typical two-family dwelling, each unit having three bedrooms. Victoria's mother's cousin, Yolanda, her husband, Frank, and their three children, Francis, Bruce and Anthony, lived upstairs. Victoria's family was on the ground floor. Their unit was laid out railroad-style, with a long hallway that led into the main living/dining area. The sparse furnishings included a comfortable pullout couch and recliner.

Victoria's father, Anthony, liked to sit in the recliner to watch old movies after everyone went to bed. When her mother was asleep, Victoria would slip out of her crib and stand in the doorway of her brothers' bedroom, knowing that her father would eventually see her.

"Hey, what are you doing there?" he'd ask.

That was her cue to climb up on his lap and snuggle in to watch along with him. Her father was her hero and protector, and a symbol of strength. Growing up, she had learned how to live, how to love, and how to recover when things didn't go right from her father.

The elder Ruvolo was a former Marine. During World War II, he had been stationed in Okinawa. It was clear to the family that Anthony's time in the armed forces had traumatized him because he never liked to share stories or speak about his service. Still, though no longer on active duty, he liked to keep a strict military schedule.

Every morning, he rose with the sun and was often out of the house before anyone was stirring.

He was handsome and powerfully built, standing exactly six feet tall. He had wavy dark hair, piercing brown eyes, and a warm, enveloping smile that never failed to comfort his daughter.

Vicky's father had come from a big family himself. He had never gone to college, but that didn't hold him back. He worked as a foreman for Bohack's, a large grocery store chain with branches scattered about the five boroughs. He also worked side jobs to bring in extra money for the family. When Vicky was born, she stayed with her parents in the master bedroom overlooking the street. When she was old enough, her parents moved her to the living room, where she shared the pullout couch with her sister, Jo-Marie. The two were closest in age and were inseparable growing up.

There was a ten year gap between the three older Ruvolo kids and the younger four. The Ruvolos had their first three children in quick succession, and for the most part, the eldest three, sisters Jeanne and Rita and brother Joey, were out of the house by the time Victoria was five.

The ten year gap between the first three Ruvolo children and the next batch was the product of the war. Anthony was called to serve in World War II after Rita's birth and the family had to be put on hold. After his return, he was plagued by horrific battlefront nightmares. Night after night, his dreams were filled with bloody, gory scenes of war with rats running rampant over the bodies on the battlefield. Some nights, he'd wake up terrified and sweating. He had trouble sleeping and spent many nights pacing the living room floor or watching TV in the old recliner.

Josephine, Victoria's mother, still wanted a big family, and eventually the children started coming again. Tommy, their second son, was born ten years after Rita. Billy was next, the youngest of the boys. Jo-Marie and Victoria finished off the brood.

Billy and Tommy shared a small walk-through room just off the living area. They had twin beds against the two walls, but everyone had to walk through their room to get to other rooms in the house, leaving very little privacy.

Continuing down the narrow hallway from the living area was a bathroom and the kitchen. Beyond the kitchen was an enclosed porch, built by Anthony. After Jeanne and Rita married and moved away, Jo-Marie and Victoria laid claim to their small bedroom off the kitchen in the back.

Anthony worked long hours, leaving the house before 6 a.m. and coming home after dark to share supper with the family. He had a solid work ethic and rarely missed a day. Even when he was sick, he'd drag himself to his job and make the best of it.

On the weekends, the family often made outings to visit relatives. In the summers, they'd escape to Rye Playland, a big amusement park in Westchester County.

Josephine was a great cook. Every Sunday she'd prepare a huge meal for the big family-day dinner. Everyone would talk at the same time, so the loudest seemed to be the one who would be heard. Josephine loved her maternal role as caregiver. Even when she was older, Victoria's mother enjoyed and loved the company of children.

Josephine Ruvolo was a traditional Italian housewife. She was good at handling the household finances and making sure her family was never wanting for anything. The house was always clean, filled with the wonderful aroma of a pot of homemade tomato sauce on the stove. She loved playing cards when she wasn't cooking or cleaning. Family card games would last for hours.

In the summers, Vicky's father would be up before sunrise and in the car for the short ride to Jones Beach. If someone was not ready when it was time to go, he'd head off anyway, leaving that person behind. Each of the kids, at one time or another, witnessed the family car disappearing around the corner with everyone but him aboard. At the beach, the family would spend the day splashing in the ocean waves and building castles in the sand. Vicky's father taught her to swim, holding her in his arms and coaxing her to kick her legs and paddle with her arms. Cousin Anthony tagged along as often as he could, making the beach outing a "more the merrier" affair.

Vicky was not a big fan of school. She was an average student who put in an average amount of effort, none of the excessive hours of homework needed to excel. She was street-smart and kind. She disliked the cliques that dictated where and how a kid would fit in socially. She was never an outcast, but she didn't like the idea of belonging to a particular group. She conscientiously selected her friends and embraced diversity. At a time when multi-culturalism was unusual, her birthday parties tended to look like meetings of the United Nations.

Vicky was thirteen when Jo-Marie and Jamesy began dating. The sisters knew him from the neighborhood. He hadn't noticed Jo-Marie until she turned sixteen and emerged from puberty as a slender, brown-haired beauty. Vicky had a crush on her sister's boyfriend, with his good looks, charm, and kindness. After their brother Billy died, Jamesy was thoughtful and attentive, and Vicky's admiration was sealed.

Victoria had been cycling through the neighborhood the day Billy died. Her mom routinely admonished her not to go far, so she never ventured further than the immediate area around the house. As she was getting ready to take a spin that afternoon, she noticed her brother when she passed through his bedroom. He was breathing more heavily than usual and seemed lethargic.

"Billy's not breathing right," she had said her mom.

But contractors were arriving soon to rebuild a bathroom, and in all the commotion, Victoria's concern was overlooked.

Once she was out on her bike, Vicky rode further than usual, going a few more blocks than were allowed by her mother. When one of the neighborhood boys came shouting after her, she assumed someone at home was upset about her disobedience. "Go home now," the boy ordered.

"Am I in trouble?" she asked.

"No, you're not in trouble. You just have to go home," he said.

As she turned the corner onto her street, she saw an ambulance crew rushing up the front walk and her mother in tears. Her mother raced out of the house to meet her on the lawn.

"Ma, what's wrong?" she implored.

Before her mother had a chance to respond, a voice rang out from the neighboring yard.

"Your brother died," someone shouted.

Suddenly, Rita's hands covered her eyes. Victoria managed to sneak a look through the space between Rita's fingers as the paramedics carried her brother down the front walkway in a body bag.

Billy had gotten mixed up with drugs and died of an overdose at the age of 19, trying what he thought was watered-down methadone. In fact, he took the drug at full strength, and it had stopped his heart.

"At night, when I lay down to close my eyes the horrible image would prevent me from falling asleep," she later recalled. "Dad comforted me when I woke up screaming, and tried as best he could to stay strong for the rest of the family. The day my brother Billy died was the first time I'd ever seen my father cry."

Each family member grieved in his own way. Josephine Ruvolo took Billy's death the hardest. She wasn't able to accept that her son was gone. Months later, she still continued to ask why Billy wasn't home yet. The rest of the family went along, hoping she'd eventually recover. The fact that Billy had been experimenting with drugs cast a stigma over his death. He had been 19 at the time, and one stupid decision had ended his life. There was no taking back his mistake, no second chance to do things differently to make his life better. Death is a consequence that can't be reversed. The whole family suffered from Billy's tragic loss for years to come.

Victoria was particularly pained that Billy's reputation was tainted by his reckless decision to get mixed up in drugs. Even then, she understood that people could make bad choices and still be good people. She was not ashamed to say that her brother had overdosed. She recognized that he had two sides, the good brother that she loved and remembered and the other brother, who had lost his fight with his demons. The cause of his death did not diminish his goodness and heart.

––––––––––––

Vicky recognized the same sort of dichotomy in Jamesy, who would eventually marry Jo-Marie and become her brother-in-law. While people in the neighborhood were scared by of his muscular build and skulking carriage, he was an angel to Vicky, coming to her emotional rescue when the world seemed to be crashing down on her.

Jamesy offered her a caring shoulder when the other members of the family were unraveling from the grief of losing Billy. She was only thirteen, and Jamesy understood that she needed a lot of support. He took her to Liberty Avenue and bought her the black dress that she wore to Billy's funeral. During the final goodbyes, he stayed at her side.

Jamesy treated Vicky like a beloved kid sister. He'd come to the house and take her on long walks, impromptu shopping sprees for clothes, and treats of ice cream at the corner store. Even though he was dating Jo-Marie, he never slighted her youngest sister.

Vicky was barely a teenager, but she was in the throes of her first crush. She was secretly infatuated with her sister's kind, incredibly handsome, warmly attentive boyfriend. She loved that she was included the day he bought a diamond engagement ring for Jo-Marie. Vicky played the role of the special confidant.

After the purchase, Vicky made Jamesy proud by not letting Jo-Marie know a thing about their secret trip to the jewelry store.

Not long after Billy's death, Vicky's father announced that he was moving the family to suburban Long Island. Crime was escalating in their Brooklyn neighborhood and Anthony wanted to move to Oceanside, a small seaside community on the Island's South Shore. He thought they would be safer and more comfortable in the suburbs. But despite her father's attempt to keep them out of harm's way, fate would have it otherwise.

Tommy was in the prime of his life. He had fallen in love with a woman named Edie, and the two of them had just moved into an apartment a few miles away from the Ruvolos' new Oceanside house.

It was 1977, and Long Island was experiencing a record snowstorm. The storm over, Tommy and Edie were driving back to their apartment when the car in front of them stopped suddenly. In an attempt to avoid hitting the vehicle, Tommy swerved into what he thought was a soft snow bank.

The snow bank, it turned out, was actually a roadblock that had become partially hidden beneath the heavy falling snow. The impact caused one of the blockade pieces to become airborne and it flew through the windshield, striking Tommy on the left side of his head.

Victoria was now seventeen years old. The call from her mother at the hospital was unforgettable. She knew from her mother's sobs that the news wasn't good.

For days, everyone anxiously awaited word on Tommy's prognosis. He had suffered a severe brain injury and doctors could do little but wait.

Tommy was just twenty-five when he died. His daughter, BilliJo, was only two. Edie and BilliJo moved into the house with Victoria and her parents, but Edie was too grief-stricken to care for her little girl. Edie moved out soon thereafter, and Vicky's parents raised their precious granddaughter as their own. For Vicky, having a toddler in the house was great fun and BilliJo became her little sister.

Vicky was twenty-one when tragedy struck the family for a third time. This time it was her brother-in-law Jamesy who was taken from them.

Married and still very much in love, Jamesy and Jo-Marie had just brought their baby boy, Billy, home from the hospital when Jamesy was murdered. His bullet-riddled body was found along the side of the Interboro Parkway in Brooklyn.

News of his murder shook everyone to the core, especially Victoria. Sadly, the murder is still unsolved and no leads have ever been made public.

With Jamesy gone, Jo-Marie and her baby son moved into the Oceanside house. Victoria now had a nephew to coddle with love, but, just as importantly, she had the company of her beloved sister. Still, she wondered if there would ever be an end to the rapid succession of family tragedies.

A year later, Victoria lost her 15-year-old nephew, Benny, Rita's son. Benny had been riding his bike home when a car struck him. The impact sent him flying over the car and he landed in the street, suffering severe injuries. He was in a coma before he finally passed away later that day.

The Ruvolos were devastated one more time. Benny had been a wonderful child, just coming into his own. When he was little, he used to deliver papers to make spending money. That Christmas, he had purchased an enormous candy cane for his Aunt Vicky, knowing how much she loved them. It had taken months to eat it, but each piece she broke off made her feel special. When her first boyfriend Dominick had proposed to her, Benny got up from the dinner table crying, telling her that he had wanted to be the one to marry her.

Victoria dreamed of having children of her own. At the age of thirty-five, she was thrilled when she found out she was pregnant. She would read to her unborn child or play music from a cassette player on her stomach. She looked forward to going to the doctor to listen to the heartbeat.

However, during her eighth-month visit to the obstetrician, her dream came to an end as she listened to the words "I can't find a heartbeat, your baby is dead."

For over a week Victoria lived in a daze, the dead fetus in her womb. When the doctors induced labor, she gave birth to a baby she named Christina. Vicky buried the baby next to her brother, Tommy, and brother-in-law, Jamesy. Although Victoria had lost her child, she never lost her maternal spirit. The love she had for Christina was transformed into a love for all children.

Victoria used poetry as an outlet for the emotions and the tragedies in her life. One of these poems, straight from her bared heart, is included here:

For Everyone Lost, April 10, 1984

> *All I have is memories*
> *of times that you spent with me*
> *days that you filled my heart*
> *with only joy and loving thoughts*
> *feelings that I never knew*
> *until the day that I found you*
> *you gave me more than words could say*
> *my thoughts of you will never fade*
> *for in my life there will always be*
> *all those sweet memories.*

CHAPTER SEVEN

> ## "An essential condition of listening to God is that the mind should not be distracted by thoughts of resentment, ill-temper, hatred or vengeance, all of which are comprised in the general term, the wrath of man."
>
> *R. V. G. Tasker, Christian author*

As I steered my car up my parents' winding driveway, I marveled at the wrought iron gazebo my mother had purchased and so enjoyed when she was healthy. When she was first diagnosed with cancer, she had hired a photographer to take a picture of the entire family dressed in black tie regalia and posing inside the whimsical structure. Growing up, I was forever amazed by her independent and positive spirit. Now, it was with a sense of dread that I parked my car next to those of my two brothers. I was relieved that they were already inside, probably visiting with my mother. More distractions, I thought to myself.

Normally, I would call my mother in between visits. But, as she had become sicker, our conversations had become less frequent. I could feel her pulling away, and that frightened me. Suddenly, I needed to hear her voice more than she needed to hear mine.

The smell of roasted chicken emanating from the kitchen reminded me of my grandmother's house on the weekends. Growing up, we would spend our Sundays in Brooklyn, visiting with my grandparents and our cousins. "The more the merrier," had always been my grandfather's mantra.

Back then, the pooper-scooper law had not yet been enacted. So without fail, my father would step out of the car into dog poop on the sidewalk.

"It's good luck," my grandfather chuckled.

My father didn't find it amusing, and usually mumbled something under his breath.

Meanwhile, the aroma of London broil, chicken soup, roast chicken and Mandel bread had us all looking forward to dinnertime.

Now as an adult, I was the one bringing my wife, Katina, and our two-year-old son, Danny, to my parents' house to dine with the family.

When my son was born, my mother was suffering from a cold and had to wear a surgical mask to view him in the hospital's nursery in the maternity ward. We had all ignored the cold because we were so busy embracing life. Now, it was impossible to ignore my mother's failing health. Her prognosis was constantly on my mind, and it drove me crazy that there was nothing I could do to help her.

"She did not have a good night," my father warned as I stepped into the kitchen, cradling my son. Everyone except my mother was seated around the kitchen island discussing her fate.

My eldest brother, Steven, was an obstetrician and gynecologist and practiced with my father, and my middle brother, David, was a pediatric infectious disease doctor conducting research at Montefiore Medical Center in the Bronx. With no real medical training, I often felt like an outsider as they employed medical terminology to discuss her condition. It was as though they were speaking a foreign language, one that I didn't understand.

I was used to this scenario, having spent many evenings around the dinner table listening to them discuss the various patients they were treating. However, I was growing less tolerant because they were no longer consulting about strangers, they were speaking about our matriarch.

My two brothers and my father had recently decided to seek a second opinion concerning her treatment because her first doctor seemed to have lost interest after her cancer reappeared.

"The result will probably be the same," my father pronounced.

"We are all focusing on her body, but what about her mind?" I said, inserting myself into the discussion.

In my studies as a psychologist, I was familiar with the research that demonstrated humans only use three percent of their brain's capability. I was also aware of the term "psycho-neuroimmunology," as discussed in Dr. John Kabat Zinn's book, *Full Catastrophe Living*. In it, he writes that, "there appear to be important interconnections, as yet poorly understood, between the brain and the immune system."

I was convinced we needed to treat my mother holistically, both her mind and body. I also believed that being surrounded by such negativity could compromise her ability to heal.

As noted in Dr. Zinn's book, there is recent research that supports the notion that there are "possible connections between stress, feelings of helplessness, immune function and diseases such as cancer."

Sensing that my suggestions were being ignored, I disappeared into the den, where I found my mother asleep on the green recliner. Our housekeeper, Filomena, was by her side, holding her hand, and monitoring her slow, shallow breaths.

During my visits to the house, I'd started to rummage through the desk in my childhood room, desperate to find letters my mother had written to me. She'd ended them all the same way, "Always have a sweet heart."

Searching for a diversion, I noticed all the newspapers for the week stacked on a shelf in the hallway. Every front cover had a story about the woman who had been struck with the frozen turkey and her amazing recovery. Grabbing a few from the stack, I disappeared into the kitchen with a sense of defiance.

"Hey Dad, did you see that the turkey lady survived the surgery?" I said, pleased to know that she had beaten the odds that my dad, the doctor, had given her. Doctors were fallible, too, though they seemed unwilling to admit it.

Although I had not met Victoria I, like the community at large, had become fascinated by her. What was it about this forty-four-year-old woman that had helped her heal so miraculously? I thought if I could share her wisdom with my mother, it would help her to heal. I secretly wished the two of them could meet.

"Yes, I saw that," my father replied. "Did you boys hear about that surgery they performed at Stony Brook Hospital? They put titanium plates in her face. Who knows how she is going to be because she had bleeding on the brain," he opined, directing his comments to the two doctors in the room.

"Rob, your mother is awake," Filomena called from the other room.

With a new sense of optimism, I walked into the den. Because I had visited with my mother daily, I wasn't able to see how much more her complexion had grayed and how her cheeks had sunk in the last couple of weeks.

"How are you doing?" I asked, flashing my best smile.

"The same," my mother replied.

I dreaded that answer. It signaled that she was becoming more resigned to her fate, and I just couldn't stomach it.

"What do you think of your new doctor?"

"If he keeps me alive, I'll like him," she responded, trying to mix a little humor into the conversation. Still, this was not like my mother, letting a doctor's opinion challenge her optimism. In the past she never would have accepted the word no, or being told, "It can't be done." That had simply made her fight harder. That's where I'd gotten my spirit from, my sense of determination. I refused to believe that something was impossible.

Nobody knows that better than my wife, Katina. I remembered when the New York Mets had agreed to my request to propose to Katina at Shea Stadium in front of a stadium full of people. My mother and I were ecstatic. But the day before the event, I received a phone call from a representative of the team informing me that they needed to cancel.

Devastated, I called in the reinforcements, my mother. I have no idea what she did, but somehow, she made the impossible happen. The Mets reversed their decision, and the next thing I knew, Katina was saying "Yes" in front of 35,000 screaming Mets fans.

"He didn't come," my mother said, lifting her head from the chair.

I didn't need to ask who she was talking about. I knew it was her brother, Barry. My mother had practically raised Barry. My grandmother had worked seven days a week, so my mother had been the one to take my Uncle Barry to see a double feature once in a while, after which they would finish off a chocolate blackout cake from Ebinger's Bakery in Brooklyn.

Now, my uncle was no longer talking to my mother because their mother, my grandmother, had changed her will and had left all of her jewelry to my mother, her only surviving daughter.

My Uncle Barry and my mother were the last living siblings. Their sister, Phyllis, had recently passed away and it was now just the two of them. My mother had been willing to give Barry some of the inherited jewelry. Even then, the two had been unable to reconcile. With the way Barry was acting, my mother felt she had lost her brother. It was clear that the conflict between the two was adding stress to her life. This stress, I believed, was interfering with her ability to heal. Their limited communication was only making the conflict deepen.

When parties are in conflict and there is no dialogue, it gives each of them an opportunity to become entrenched in the belief that he is right. The adversarial approach in the legal system is the same. When a person retains an attorney, the first advice he is given is to make sure that he doesn't talk to the other party. This lack of communication diminishes the likelihood of healing the relationship. The opportunity for my mother and her brother to heal their divide was slipping away.

CHAPTER EIGHT

> ## "Only a kind person is able to judge another justly and to make allowances for his weaknesses. A kind eye, while recognizing defects, sees beyond them."

Reverend Lawrence G. Lovasik, Divine Word Missionary

Unsure of how Victoria would cope with learning what had happened to her, Rita and Jo-Marie decided to hold off telling her the details of the incident until she was physically stronger. Besides, Victoria's injuries had left her with very poor short-term memory. She tended to forget most of what she'd been told within a few hours. They would wait for the psychologist on staff at St. Charles Hospital to be present when they delivered the news.

Jo-Marie and Rita were both there the day that psychologist Debra

Smith and Semel-Concepcion, M.D. came to speak with Vicky. Sitting in chairs around her hospital bed, the two doctors calmly spoke to her about her ordeal.

"Vicky, your accident happened because some teenagers threw a turkey out of their car and it hit your windshield," one of the doctors began.

There was a momentary silence as Victoria pulled herself up in bed, contemplating what she had just learned. Then, to the surprise of the doctors in the room, she asked a question about her assailants, not herself.

"Well, do they realize they have ruined their lives as much as they ruined mine?" she asked. "These kids really made such a stupid mistake." Intuitively, Victoria knew that the actions of these teens were not about her.

We assume that when harm occurs, the act of harming must be about us. In most cases, this is not true. People tend to take their own negativity and transfer it onto someone else. In turn, that person responds in a negative way and the hostile cycle continues. The realization that it is not about "you" frees a person from feeling that he has an obligation to respond.

———————

After several weeks of grueling rehab at St. Charles, Victoria was ready to go home. It was only because she was taking OxyContin, one of the strongest painkillers on the market, that she agreed to go to Rita's house in Oceanside.

Hospital administrators had never held a press conference in the hospital lobby for the discharge of a patient. However, because of the public interest, Victoria's family agreed that a press conference would be the best way to express its gratitude and respond to the innumerable questions that it had been getting from reporters and producers.

This was the first time that the media and public would actually get to see Vicky since the crash. No one had seen her when she was discharged from Stony Brook and taken to St. Charles.

The hospital lobby was packed when the nurse pushed the wheelchair into the lobby. Vicky was photographed that day dressed in a pink terry cloth jump suit and holding a stuffed teddy bear.

She held up a sign that read, "Thank You," as Jim O'Connor, the executive director of the hospital read her very brief statement: "These past weeks have been very difficult, but the outpouring of love, support, and prayers have helped so much in my recovery."

She also had a special thank you for Louis Erali, "You saved my life."

Not surprisingly, Vicky's tragic encounter with the frozen turkey and her recovery continued to spread outside Long Island and the State of New York. Cards and letters from well-wishers continued to pour in from around the country.

Dear Victoria,

I heard of your terrible experience on the news, and I would like to extend to you my deepest sadness. The incident was most unfair and unfortunate. Please know that people countrywide know of your story and are rooting for you.

Regards Sue W., Norwich CT

Rita and Ben's house was immaculate and quiet, which is why Victoria chose to stay there. With their children grown and out of the house, there was not much activity during the day. Ben, who she quickly nicknamed Dr. Ben Casey after the television character from the 1960's medical drama of the same name, elected to be responsible for her care. Every night, Ben would clean the surgical incision in his sister-in-law's neck where the trach tube had been.

In the beginning, Vicky was tired and slept a lot. But as she began to gain strength, she found it increasingly difficult to sit still. She grew tired of the peace and quiet afforded by her temporary sanctuary.

After only a few weeks, Vicky decided to move in with her sister

Jo-Marie, her husband, Jimmy, and their children, Billy and Jillian.

At first, fourteen-year-old Jillian welcomed her aunt and was happy to have her at the house. The two had a great relationship, and Jillian saw Vicky as her hip relative and the woman who regularly took her to concerts and other fun activities. Jillian also knew that Aunt Vicky was very independent.

Now, after the incident, Jillian realized that there was little that her aunt could do on her own, that she often repeated herself, and she was almost childlike in her deportment. Vicky's behavior deeply disturbed Jillian.

Jillian found herself dealing with a mix of emotions. She felt guilty and partly responsible for inviting her aunt to her performance and having her on the road that fateful night, and she was also frustrated with Vicky's incapacity. Jillian would shout in anger at her aunt when she repeated herself, and then feel guilty that she'd done so. She was still quite young and didn't really understand how deeply affected she'd been by what had happened.

Victoria was only now learning that Jillian had been blaming herself for the incident. "If I wasn't performing that night, you would never have come out in that weather," Jillian told her aunt.

It was a heartbreaking moment for Victoria. Her niece had done nothing wrong; it wasn't her fault that Ryan tossed the turkey out of the car. Fate had put Vicky on that section of Portion Road as Ryan and his friends drove by in the opposite direction. But, like many people who assume guilt, Jillian believed that she was somehow at fault and responsible. Her guilt had been mixed and confused with anger at Ryan and the other teens for weeks.

Jillian also confided that she had wanted to exact revenge against Ryan Cushing and his friends. She harbored so much anger that she'd thought about getting a group of her friends together to beat all of them up. Fortunately, she never acted on her thoughts. "Perhaps my being there was to save someone else's life," Vicky told her.

During adolescence, kids often lash out at the ones they love the most because of difficulty verbalizing their emotions. We tell our kids that if they are good, then good things will happen to them. Part of growing up is learning that this is not always the case; the reciprocity is not perfectly clear-cut.

Jillian was seeing someone she adored, someone who had always been strong, become weak before her own eyes. To make matters worse, Jillian thought she was the cause of Victoria's injuries. Understandably, Jillian was acting out at anyone who stood in her way, exercising what is properly called displaced anger. Ironically, it was Victoria who often received her wrath. What we can learn from this is that when our children lash out at us, they are waving a red flag that says 'this is not necessarily about you. This is me telling you that I am having trouble coping with the unfairness in life.' Our role is to listen and to provide guidance to help them deal with this frustration in a more productive way.

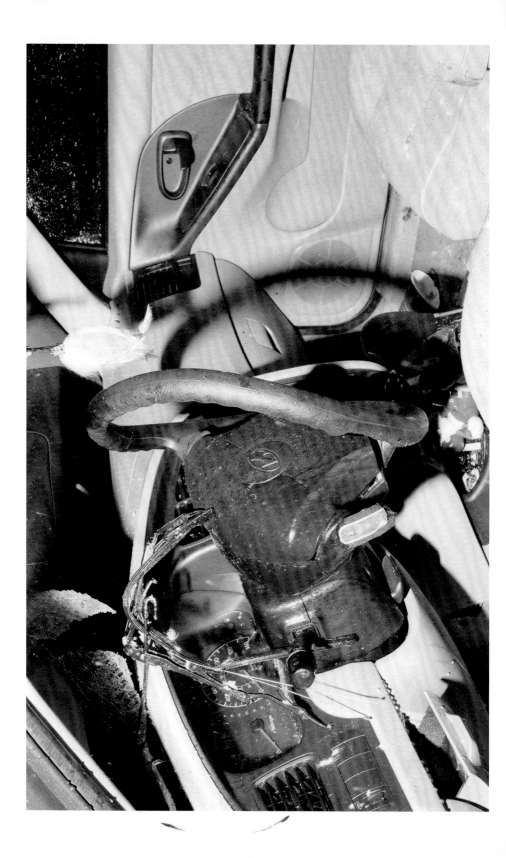

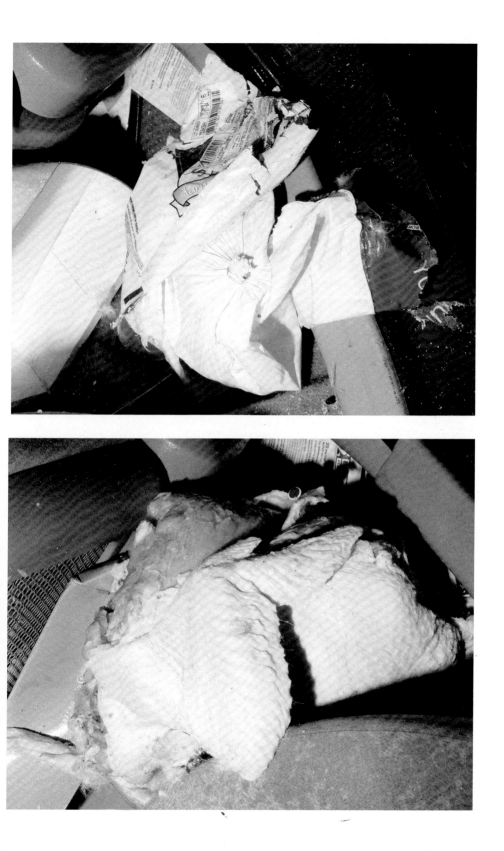

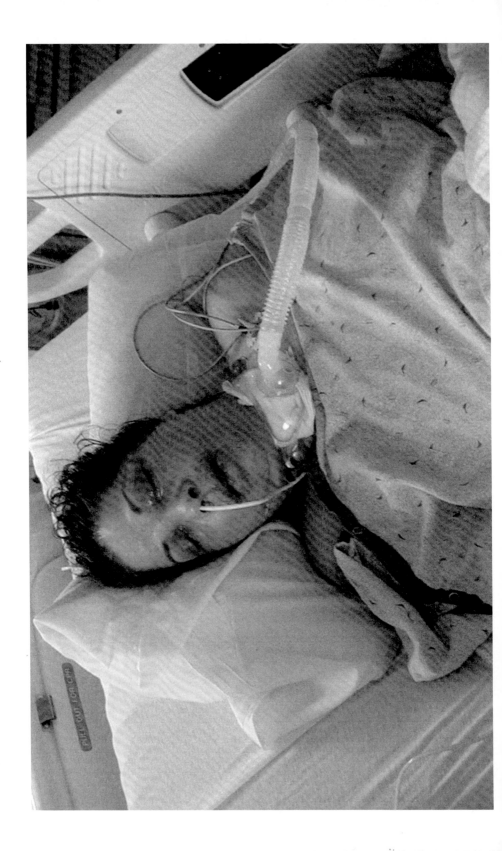

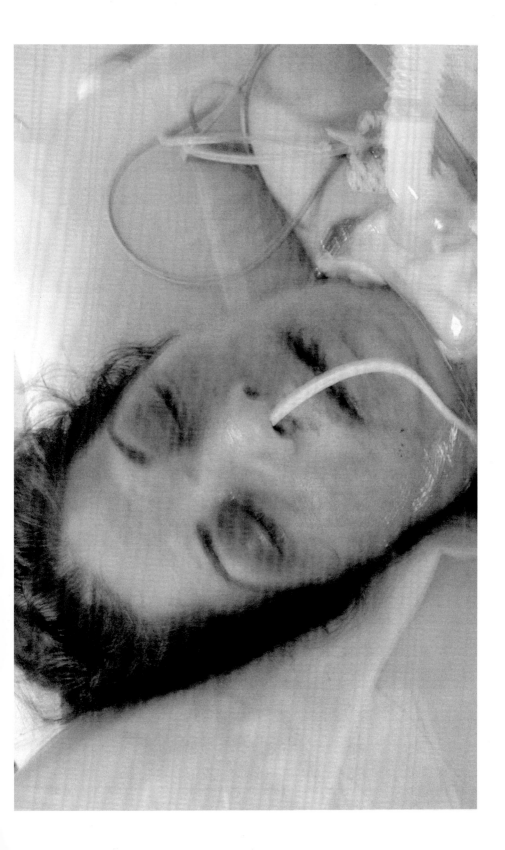

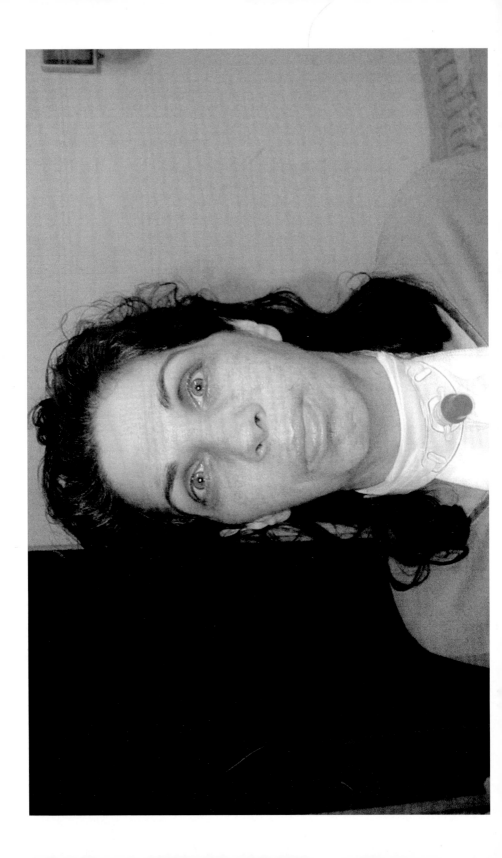

CHAPTER NINE

| "Vengeance has no foresight." |

Napoleon Bonaparte

I t was a cold winter day in late January 2005 when Victoria and her family drove out to Riverhead, the county seat toward the eastern end of Long Island, to meet with the members of the Suffolk County District Attorney's Office who had been assigned to prosecute her case.

This was longest trip she'd taken since leaving rehab at St. Charles Hospital. The meeting got underway, with Assistant District Attorney Nancy Clifford and the D.A.'s Bureau Chief, Peter Mayer, going over the particulars. Vicky was in serious pain; her head and face were pounding in discomfort. But she didn't want to complain. She was determined to attend this meeting.

Victoria had been taking OxyContin, but she didn't like the constant groggy state. So, she had stopped the medication only ten days prior to this meeting.

"How are you feeling?" asked Mayer.

"I am just happy to be alive," she said with gratitude.

While Vicky was physically present for the meeting, her mind tended to wander. This was the largest number of people that she'd been with since her injury, and she was feeling overwhelmed by the new surroundings. Her eyes wandered from one business suit to another. She let her sisters do the talking.

"This bunch needs to pay for what they did," Jo-Marie said.

Vicky's sister had said the very same thing years earlier when her first husband, Jamesy, was murdered. But his killers were still at large. Jo-Marie wanted to make sure she saw justice this time, and in her mind that meant punishing the kids who were responsible to the fullest extent of the law.

Rita had also seen the toll Ryan's act had taken on Vicky. She'd witnessed her sister's suffering and remained concerned that she was still at risk for having a seizure. Doctors had warned that there remained a risk for these complications up to six months after her injuries.

Victoria injuries had created casualties beyond her personal condition. There was Louis, who had seen the shattered glass piercing her face as he coasted the car to safety. He was filled with rage over what had happened to his dear friend. He wanted those kids to pay. Vicky thought, too, about all her pets who had suffered quietly while she was in the hospital and rehab. Months later, she heard how people she had never met were afraid to drive a car after hearing what had befallen her.

Victoria's sisters, Jo-Marie and Rita, and their husbands, Ben and Jimmy, were adversely affected. Jo- Marie suffered from nightmares of the deformed face she'd seen that first night at the hospital when staff members warned her that her sister might die. She also was angry that while Vicky appeared to be healing on the surface, she was not the same. Jo-Marie had to constantly remind Vicky of the close relationship they had once shared.

"Is there any way we can sit down with Ryan and ask him what he was thinking?" Rita asked. For years, Rita had wanted to confront the driver who had struck and killed her son Benny. She and her husband had never recovered from losing their fifteen-year-old son. His death had been ruled an accident. While the driver had remained at the scene until police arrived, he had never reached out to the family to apologize for their loss. For Rita and her husband, losing their precious Benny Boy had been incomprehensible.

"No, he has lawyers and his lawyers speak for him," responded Assistant District Attorney Clifford.

Constant, heavy pain often makes a person feel exhausted, and Victoria was no exception. During the meeting, she was too weak to become a part of the conversation, even though she desperately wanted to.

"I am sorry. I am not feeling well. Can we meet again later to discuss this, when I am up to it?" she asked.

"Sure, just take care of yourself," the prosecutor said.

———————————

Victoria was more lucid the second time she met with Clifford and Mayer, on February 27. Her family was there once again for moral support. But, she felt strong enough to represent herself in this meeting, and she had come armed with a series of questions.

"Vicky, we are happy to let you know that we have remained strong in our prosecution of the case and have not budged from our offer of twenty-five years for Mr. Cushing," Clifford said confidently.

"What about the other kids who were there with him that night?" Vicky asked. "My father always said that when you are with your friends and they do something wrong, you are just as guilty."

"We won't be able to get twenty-five years on them," he said. "They have pled to various crimes and will, in all likelihood, be sentenced to probation."

"A slap on the wrist!" Victoria said. "But they all left me to die on the roadside that night."

"We need all of their testimony in the event we go to trial against Ryan," Clifford said.

"What did the driver say?"

"He said he tried to stop Ryan from throwing the turkey out the window," Clifford responded.

"Then why didn't he stop the car or roll up the windows?" Vicky asked.

In reality, Victoria's questions were excellent, a bit painful for the prosecutors to respond to, but pertinent nonetheless. In fact, Clifford and Mayer had asked those very same questions themselves. But they'd decided that they wanted to build a strong case against the one individual who was most at fault in the incident, Ryan Cushing. In return, they were willing to let the other teens take lesser pleas. It didn't seem right, but it was a reality of the plea bargain system.

There was another unspoken undercurrent for the prosecutors in this case, too. The media, not just local media but the national media as well, were providing extensive coverage of Victoria's story. Suffolk County District Attorney Thomas Spota would want the prosecution to be able to file serious charges against at least one of the four teens and make those charges stick.

"Vicky, we feel that Ryan is the person most responsible for hurting you and if it means making deals with the other kids, then we have no choice," Mayer said.

"What can you tell me about Ryan?" Vicky asked.

"He recently got in trouble for throwing eggs at his girlfriend's house. But he does not have a criminal record. Ryan is legally blind and his parents are divorced," Clifford said. "Ryan's father recently left his mother for another woman."

"Well, why didn't he throw the turkey at her? I didn't take his father." Vicky joked. "What are the options that Ryan can get?"

"In all likelihood, we can get twenty-five years if we go to trial," Mayer explained.

"But how is putting him behind bars for twenty-five years going to teach him anything?" Vicky wanted to know.

Jo-Marie was whispering something in the advocate's ear. Then, turning to her sister, she suddenly yelled, "Vicky, he almost killed you!"

"I will always remember what happened to me," Vicky responded. "But he will hide behind bars and come out as the hardened criminal we believe him to be."

"Vicky, Ryan can do up to twenty-five years but we have the discretion to offer what we feel is appropriate," interjected Mayer.

Vicky wanted more time to process the possibilities.

"I don't know, can I think more about this before I tell you what I want?"

Victoria left the District Attorney's office with passionate determination to return to independent living and continued healing.

CHAPTER TEN

"Something of vengeance I had tasted for the first time; as aromatic wine it seemed, on swallowing, warm and racy; its after-flavor, metallic and corroding, gave me a sensation as if I had been poisoned."

Charlotte Bronte

Voir dire, translated from Old French as "to speak the truth," is used by our legal system to describe the process of posing a series of questions to potential jurors in order to weed out those who are unable to sit as a juror because they have already prejudged the case. For some lawyers this process is something to be taken seriously and logically; other lawyers would be content to just select the first twelve people whose names were randomly called first.

In my role of combining my legal and psychological skills, I was at the Suffolk County courthouse in Riverhead assisting a colleague with a voir dire, jury selection in a civil trial, when my cell phone rang. It was my eldest brother, Steven.

"Rob, make sure you stop at Mom's for lunch," he instructed me.

I could feel the blood drain from my head as Steven's words sank in. As my mother's cancer continued to spread, she grew too weak to talk on the phone, so I relied on others for her medical updates.

"Is she okay?"

"She's having a tough time breathing this morning, but she is resting now and should feel better when she wakes up," Steven said with an air of optimism. Still, I could tell by the tightness in his voice that he was concerned.

During my mother's illness, I had grown closer to both of my brothers, Steven and David. As I was the youngest of the three, perhaps they were still trying to protect me.

When jury selection resumed, I was useless to my colleague. I could not focus on the action in court that day. All I could think of was my mother lying on the green recliner as she struggled between breaths.

"I am sorry, I have to leave. My mom is not feeling well," I told my colleague.

Not waiting for a response, I grabbed my briefcase and left the courtroom without another word. I walked quickly to the parking lot and sped off in my car. I kept telling myself that my mother would feel stronger when she woke up. I had no idea how I found my way from Riverhead to Oakdale; I don't remember making the twenty-minute drive. As I pulled into the driveway, I saw the front door to our house was open and my brother Steven was standing just inside the storm door. We were in the middle of winter and the temperatures had dipped into the 20's, yet he stepped outside without a jacket to meet me as I made my way up the walkway. I wondered why he wasn't sitting with Mom. Maybe she was still sleeping?

"Rob, Mom is dead," he said in a gentle voice. His words hit me like a cold slap.

I had not prepared myself for this moment. I knew that my mother was terminally ill and that she would die. Still, I had somehow convinced myself that this day would never come.

Devastated, I fell to my knees into the heavy mixture of snow and sleet that covered the ground. I felt unbearable anger as I grabbed a handful of the frozen sleet and hurled it across the yard.

"No!" I wailed, praying I would wake myself up from this nightmare.

I ran past my brother into the house. My father was in the kitchen. His eyes were glazed and bloodshot, and he held his head in his hands. Filomena was sitting at the long dining table, staring out the window.

"Rob, your mother is still in the room. Go and see her," she urged.

I was not emotionally prepared for this task. I suppose that no one ever is. I walked into the den and was shocked to see her gray complexion, which matched the color of her tousled hair. Getting down on my knees beside her, I held her icy hands and cried.

Suddenly, I was overcome with anger. I thought of my Uncle Barry. In my grief, I had convinced myself that his failure to visit my mother had hastened her death. Grabbing the cordless phone from the table, I dialed my mother's only brother, the one who had been fighting with her over my grandmother's jewelry. I was angry that in spite of their bitter feelings, he had not once come to make amends during the time she had been sick.

My aunt answered the phone. Unlike her husband, she had made the short trip from Bay Shore to Oakdale to sit by my mother's bedside. But it did not matter. I could feel my heart racing, and I had only one thought, to cause Barry pain and regret.

"Guess where I am?" I asked. There was silence on the other end of the phone.

"I am here sitting with my dead mother, you bitch!" I yelled. I did not care what her response was going to be. I just wanted her to hear the rage in my voice. "I hope you and Uncle Barry are happy. Don't even think about coming to the funeral."

When I was ten years old, I attended my first funeral with my mother. I remember her wiping my tears as she told me, "Funerals are not important; what matters is that you were good to the person when they were alive."

There was no one to wipe my tears now as I hung up the phone. Leaving my mother's side, I returned to the kitchen to tell my brother and father what I had done. They were shocked but sympathetic.

Knowing my mother would have been disappointed in me for making that call to her brother and for the way I had spoken to my aunt, I later called them back to apologize. This time, I talked to my uncle. In a calm tone, I explained to him why I did not want him to come to the funeral. Even though my anger toward him was really anger that my mother had died, I wasn't able to acknowledge this at the time. My aunt attended the funeral, but my uncle did not.

I was in a state of shock dealing with the loss of my mother, my best friend, and I continued to take out my anger on anyone who crossed my path for days after her death. I was short with my wife; I had no patience for my son, Danny. I would not want my young son acting this way, but I behaved badly in spite of myself.

Since first reading about Victoria's harrowing ordeal, I had believed that if I could somehow introduce her to my mother, the meeting might help my mother heal. It was then that I realized the one who needed to meet her was me.

CHAPTER ELEVEN

> "Kindness and giving is the best way. You get so much more out of life when you give."

Victoria Ruvolo

Victoria went for an outpatient consultation to determine what physical and occupational therapy she would require. She could not lift either of her feet, which made her shuffle as she walked. Also, the right side of her face sagged above her lip. She was placed on a regimen of physical therapy once a week for a month. The nerves in her face would require time to regenerate on their own. When they did, Victoria found herself in excruciating pain. To this day, she can predict if it is going to rain by the pain in her face.

But, this was neither the eighteen months of rehabilitation nor the full-time aid that the doctors had thought she would need. She had truly defied the odds and amazed everyone by her quick recovery.

For Victoria, however, her recovery was not fast enough. It had been four months from the night she went to see her niece perform and she was still not home. No time was wasted on thoughts of punishing the kids who caused all this suffering. The only thing Victoria focused on was being well enough to go home.

"Bob was a big boy," Vicky said aloud to no one in particular. The phrase was a tiny part of her ongoing physical therapy, designed to restore strength in her facial muscles and improve her speech.

"Who are you talking to?" asked Jo-Marie.

"Nobody. I am doing my exercises."

Jo-Marie was trying to do everything she could for her sister, and indeed, she'd provided a safe, caring environment. But Vicky missed her independence. She wanted to be home with her pets, and she didn't want to be under a microscope with her sister watching and worrying about her every move.

So far as Jo-Marie was concerned, Vicky had to prove to her that she was truly okay before she would let her leave. If that meant making her bed and offering to set the table for dinner, then Vicky would do so.

"Vicky, you set the table with breakfast glasses and it's dinner time," Jo-Marie said.

In reality, Vicky had never made much of a distinction between juice glasses for breakfast and regular glasses for dinner. But for Jo-Marie, it was a warning that her sister was not ready to be on her own, or at least that's what she said.

In her heart, Jo-Marie was afraid to let Vicky go home because it was still possible for her to have a seizure. The risk would be there for another few months.

Finally, during the second week in April, Vicky was strong enough to move back to Ronkonkoma, five-and-a-half months after the incident and well short of the eighteen months of rehabilitation that the doctors had predicted. But her heartache and pain weren't over yet. While she had been in the hospital, one of her four beloved cats, Mittens, had passed away. The friend, David Moore, who'd been so thoughtful in caring for her animals, had done everything he could to try to save the feline, but to no avail. Learning of the cat's passing was a devastating emotional setback for her.

In the quiet of her own home, Vicky also had more of a chance to reflect on what had happened to her and what lay ahead for both her and her assailant, Ryan.

When she was at Jo-Marie's, Victoria could not decipher how she felt. She wasn't angry. Rather, she was frustrated. She wanted to get back home and get on with her life. On some days, she would speculate about Ryan's life in jail. "Let's see how well he would do in prison. I wonder if he will feel like a big shot there!" she would say.

Jo-Marie wanted the maximum punishment for Ryan, for him to spend his adult life in jail. But for Vicky, the decision was not cut-and-dried. She found it impossible to sort through her feelings. She was anxious to return home, where she would have time to think things through for herself.

———————

Vicky was learning more about Ryan through members of the D.A.'s office, and the more she learned, the more compassion she felt for him. She wondered if her sense of concern for Ryan could be traced back to her own childhood and her parents' determination to be there for their children, no matter what the circumstances. She did not see much of a support system for Ryan and could not imagine what it would be like to not have a parent to turn to for help.

She also had to consider the physical and emotional pain that had been thrust upon her, and the months she had lost in recovery and healing. "I'm the one who will feel it for the rest of my life," she considered as she weighed the pros and cons of harsh justice.

Still, she could not stop caring about Ryan and she ultimately decided that extensive jail time was not what she wanted for him. Instead, she wanted to offer him help. Extending a hand to the underdog had always been in her nature.

———————

Not long after she made her decision, Vicky talked to attorney Paul Feur to discuss the case against Ryan. She had previously decided to file civil proceedings against Ryan and his family for monetary damages to cover the financial losses she'd sustained from her injuries. She had thousands of dollars in expenses with no way to cover them. And physically, she was not well enough to return to work.

Vicky had complete trust in Feur, who had been an assistant district attorney himself. She needed some guidance on how to deal with Ryan and the criminal justice system from someone other than a family member. She didn't want Ryan to be sent to a prison somewhere upstate; she preferred that he serve his sentence locally.

She also believed that having Ryan on probation for an extended period of time after jail would do him good in the long run. This way, he would still be accountable for his actions. If he did something criminal and stupid again, he would certainly find himself going to prison for a long time.

If Ryan agreed to a plea bargain, the shortest allowable jail time was six months, with a five-year mandatory probation.

"I really believe that's what makes sense for me," she finally decided.

"Vicky, you need to do what you feel is right for you," Feur advised.

Later that evening, Victoria sat down with her sister, Jo-Marie, to tell her that she'd made up her mind. She was intending to ask the D.A.'s office to drop its push for a lengthy jail term and give Ryan a lengthy probation instead.

"You really do have a head injury," Jo-Marie told Vicky on hearing the news.

"Well, it is what I want and what I can live with," Vicky responded, confident in her decision.

CHAPTER TWELVE

"It is the confession, not the priest, that gives us absolution."

Oscar Wilde

N ine months after the accident, Victoria returned to her job at the collection agency, making every attempt to bring her life back to normal. But the court date for Ryan's plea was scheduled for the fifteenth of August 2005, and family and friends worried about how she would fare when she faced her attacker in court.

The Riverhead courthouse was in the same building where Victoria and her family had held their previous meetings with prosecutors Nancy Clifford and Pete Meyer. Victoria and her family made their way through the scanners and onto the elevator to the second floor.

Victoria was curious to finally see the young man who was responsible for causing her so much pain and for whom she had advocated. But first, she had to negotiate the feeding frenzy of media representatives crowded in the hallway. In New York State, only reporters are allowed in the courtroom, not cameramen or cameras. The cameramen and their news crews were lined and waiting along the hall outside Judge Barbara Kahn's courtroom.

"Here they come!" one them yelled.

As she rushed toward the courtroom assigned to her case, Victoria saw the cameramen jump to their feet. She stared straight ahead, avoiding eye contact.

"Could all this commotion be for my case?" she asked herself.

Judge Kahn was not yet on the bench, but the courtroom was packed with news reporters, attorneys, and curious onlookers. The court officers had reserved the second row for Victoria and her family. Victoria took the seat closest to the aisle. Filling the row were Victoria's two sisters, their husbands, and her nieces Jillian and Billy Jo, all there to support her. None of them, especially Jo-Marie, had been able to fully comprehend her decision to be moderate with Ryan's punishment. All anxiously awaited his arrival, curious to see if he fit the impression each had of him.

Each time the door was opened, Jillian would ask if the person coming in was Ryan. Jillian only knew what he looked like from the pictures she'd seen in the newspaper. They tended to depict him in a negative way, with a snide smile or squinty eyes. Based on the images she'd seen, Jillian had prejudged Ryan, assuming he must be a bully, like the ones she knew in her school.

Jo-Marie sat next to Vicky, contemplating all that had happened to her sister and what still lay ahead. Very few people in the courtroom that day had any comprehension of the pain and trauma that Vicky had experienced. They didn't know the details of her surgery or the extent of her ongoing agonizing discomfort.

Jo-Marie thought about her sister's hospital bills that had been accumulating at home and the many nights Rita and she had spent away from their own families to care for their sister. She remembered the nights she spent worrying that Vicky might never wake from the coma. She knew her sister was still struggling to remember things from their childhood. The idea that her sister was not going to make someone "pay" for this was troubling her.

Benny sat quietly next to Vicky. He, too, questioned his sister-in-law's decision to ask for leniency, although he never expressed his reservations to her. Still, he was envious of Vicky's spirit. His thoughts turned to his own tragedy, when he had lost Benny Boy. For years, he had been living with unrelenting rage directed toward the motorist who had struck and killed his child. He realized that his rage was haunting him and keeping him from moving forward. Taking care of Vicky, he admired her ability to avoid dwelling on the past, and he hoped that her determination to focus on the future would rub off on him. As he had witnessed her heal and resume her job that August, he began to understand the importance of letting go. He wanted to start putting his own anger behind him.

Suffolk County District Attorney Thomas Spota quietly entered the courtroom and sat in the back row. Back in December he had told a *Daily News* reporter, "Ryan...was the ring leader and the direct cause of the horrendous injuries. For that he has to pay a penalty - a significant one."

Now, Ryan was going to get off lightly because Vicky Ruvolo, as the victim, had impact on the sentence, and she wanted it to be light. Spota had some reservations about that plea deal. Suffolk County's residents had voted him into office partly because he had a reputation as a tough prosecutor. He'd already told Vicky that he thought she was being too easy on Ryan.

The D.A. wondered what would happen if Ryan were to run afoul of the law a second time. Would Suffolk's residents blame him or Vicky for treating Ryan so charitably?

Spota's reputation and credibility were on the line. It would have been easier to ignore Vicky's petitions and allow the case to take its natural course. Normally, victim impact statements strive to elicit maximum sentences, so Vicky's case was highly unusual. Still, he had faith in the Assistant District Attorneys, Nancy Clifford and Pete Mayer, and he wanted Victoria's wishes honored.

Clifford strode into the courtroom a few minutes later with a look of determination and confidence. The petite brunette walked past the rows of onlookers and sat at the prosecution table next to

Bureau Chief Mayer. Clifford knew the facts of her case and was confident in her position. She glanced over her shoulder and smiled at Vicky and her family. She was amazed at how the family was always there supporting Vicky. In contrast, Ryan seemed to come alone, accompanied only by his attorneys to all the court proceedings.

Ryan entered the courtroom flanked by his lawyers.

"That can't be him," said Jillian, as she glanced over her shoulder at her mother. "He didn't look like that in the newspapers."

Ryan was wearing a grey pinstriped suit that seemed to swallow his slender body. He walked with a slow gait and looked down, avoiding eye contact with the gallery.

"Mom, how could he even have had the strength to lift a turkey?" Jillian whispered.

As Ryan came closer, Jillian stared at him. This was not the individual she had imagined. How had she perceived him to be so different from the frail and frightened-looking boy standing in front of her? Focusing more on him, her feelings started to soften. Before, she had been feeling rage and hatred; now, empathy was creeping in. Jillian realized that Ryan might have issues that deserved consideration. Maybe he had low self-esteem and wanted to do something stupid in an effort to earn friends, despite the consequences. She wondered if he'd been tormented by bullies like she'd been.

Jo-Marie also observed Ryan as he walked to his place at the defense table. She was equally surprised that she didn't see the monster who had stared out from the photographs in the newspapers, but a regular teenager, at the moment dressed in an oversized suit. Jo-Marie had two children of her own and understood as much as anybody that children make mistakes. But, she'd never been able to picture Ryan as any age but that of full-fledged adult until that moment.

Ryan sat down at the defense table with his lawyers, Vincent Trimarco and William Keahon.

Benny was lost in thought. He seemed to be looking at the back of Ryan's thin neck, he was actually thinking about the man who had tragically ended Benny Boy's life.

"How could I give that driver so much power over me?" Benny was asking himself. His eyes began to water as he realized how much time he had wasted in his anger. His rage over his son's death kept him imprisoned in grief and anger. Benny vowed to himself that if Vicky was able to move forward, he would try to do the same.

"All rise, the Honorable Judge Barbara Kahn presiding," the court clerk declared.

Kahn had presided over many of the court appearances in the case against Ryan.

"Number one on the calendar, for the conference in the matter of Ryan Cushing," the clerk bellowed. Ryan and his attorneys stepped forward toward the rail facing the judge, as did as ADA Clifford and Bureau Chief Mayer.

"Good morning," the judge began. "It is my understanding that there is a proposed disposition of this matter. Would the People care to place that on the record?"

"Yes, your honor, it is my understanding that the defendant offers to withdraw the previously entered plea of not guilty and in its place instead enter a plea of guilty to Assault in the Second Degree. The prepared plea is coupled with a proposed sentence subject to the approval of the Court of a period of incarceration of no greater than six months with period of probation no greater than five years," Mr. Mayer said.

Victoria had succeeded in making her own case for justice and Judge Kahn was willing to consider her wishes. But she wanted to make sure that the court record was clear, so that no one would later question the court's motive. "Mr. Mayer, as part of what you're outlining as a proposed disposition, place on the record the reasons for the People's recommendation," she instructed.

"Your Honor, the case as you know involves this defendant on November 13, 2004, at about 12:30 am throwing a 20.5 pound turkey out a window, hitting the windshield of a car operated by Ms. Victoria Ruvolo who was a victim in this case," Mr. Mayer explained. "She is present here with members of her family."

"Ms. Clifford, who is to my right, and myself as well as the District Attorney have spent some time, and I must say Ms. Clifford and myself particularly, in the investigation of this case in consultation with Ms. Ruvolo and her family. The first thing I am happy to report is that she recovered remarkably from this. But there is no question that the results of Mr. Cushing's behavior were overwhelmingly egregious. Having said that, our normal posture in a case like this would be to insist on state prison. Ms. Ruvolo has recovered remarkably. She is a remarkable individual. She has always taken the position with us that she didn't wish excessive punitive measures with respect to this defendant. It is also very clear, your Honor, that based upon a very extensive investigation both prior to and subsequent to the grand jury proceedings by Ms. Clifford and myself that it's clear to us that Mr. Cushing never intended or expected the egregious results that occurred here. But his conduct was purely reckless, as that term is defined in the penal law, in that he created a substantial and unjustifiable risk of serious physical injury or death, was aware of the risk and consciously disregarded it.

"Notwithstanding that fact, we've also looked very extensively at Mr. Cushing's background. There are some mitigating factors in there that we have considered that Mr. Keahon has submitted on his behalf. But by and large, we are proposing to consent to the proposal made by Mr. Keahon, predicated on our lengthy discussions with Ms. Ruvolo.

"Judge, it took us a while to conclude that justice would be served in this case under all the circumstances with the proposal that we are making to the Court. And I think I can tell you unequivocally, this coupled with Ms. Ruvolo's thoughts and recommendations and her sensitivity, as well as the available evidence, which has convinced us that Mr. Cushing's behavior, while reckless, also demonstrates that he did not intend or expect these terrible consequences. For all these reasons, your Honor, we are recommending that the Court accept the proposed disposition," Mr. Mayer said.

The judge asked the defense attorney, Mr. Keahon, if he had

anything to add. In criminal proceedings, the defense is always given the opportunity to be heard. Under the adversarial system, it is anticipated that this time is reserved for the defendant to rebut or clarify his position. However, this was not a typical proceeding.

"Yes Judge, I join in the application and comments and statement made by Mr. Mayer," Mr. Keahon said. "And I would like to add that I know that this disposition would never take place or be offered by the District Attorney's Office or be considered by the Court as the disposition in this case without the compassion shown by Ms. Ruvolo, who I believe all of us from the bench on down have hoped and prayed for a speedy and full recovery."

Looking back at Vicky, Keahon continued, "I see her in the courtroom and I thank you so much. I have been practicing law for 32 years both as a prosecutor and defense attorney. I have never seen in those 32 years, a victim, a true victim, who has suffered, shown the compassion, the forgiveness. There must be a tremendous amount of spirituality in your life."

Vicky nodded but offered no comment. As she sat observing the proceedings, she wondered if Ryan had the physical and emotional strength to survive his six-month stint in jail. Either way, Vicky thought he needed to go to jail, albeit briefly, so that he'd understand what it was like to lose his freedom. Perhaps his time behind bars would help ensure that he'd think twice before doing something stupid again.

Ryan Cushing was still a teenager, a skinny young man in body and an adolescent in mind. He was emotionally immature and had certainly screwed up, badly. Cushing's wrongdoings required consequences, but not to the extent the community and the Suffolk County D.A.'s office were looking for. Sending Ryan to prison for twenty years would have ruined him and potentially turned him into an angry, resentful man with a chip on his shoulder, very limited skills, and the wrong kind of friends and contacts. A hard prison sentence for Ryan would also have done nothing to help Vicky move ahead and heal.

Ryan was asked to step forward to make an allocution, a statement of the facts in the case, before the judge. It was the first opportunity for Ryan to speak publicly about the night he had nearly killed Victoria. Mayer oversaw that portion of the proceeding.

"Mr. Cushing, I'm going to ask you some questions about the events that occurred on November 12 and 13, 2004," Mayer said. "I'm going to call your attention back now to late evening November 12, and the early morning hours, November 13. At about that time, were you traveling in a car on Portion Road in Ronkonkoma, Town of Brookhaven, Suffolk County, New York?"

"Yes," Ryan whispered.

"Where were you seated?" the prosecutor asked.

"I was sitting in the back seat."

"What did you have with you in the back seat?" Mayer continued.

"A turkey."

"And did you buy that turkey a short while earlier at Waldbaum's in Ronkonkoma? Mayer inquired.

"Yes," Ryan said.

"And while you were traveling in Jack's car did there come a time that you decided to throw the turkey out the rear driver's side window?"

"Yes," Ryan acknowledged.

"You agree therefore, Mr. Cushing, that the act of throwing that turkey which you did in the early morning hours of November 13 under these sets of circumstances was a reckless act?"

"Yes," Ryan said again, as tears rolled down his cheeks.

"Did you learn the turkey smashed Ms. Ruvolo's windshield, struck her in the face?" Mayer continued.

"Yes."

"Are the People satisfied with this allocution?" asked Judge Kahn.

"Yes," answered Mayer.

"Mr. Cushing, with respect to the crime of Assault in the Second Degree, in violation of Penal Law 120.05 subdivision 4, how do you plead: guilty or not guilty?" asked the Judge.

"Guilty," Ryan responded.

The prosecution never asked Ryan why he'd thrown the turkey. From the prosecution's perspective, at least, it didn't matter. There probably was no satisfactory answer. Ryan had acknowledged what he'd done, and that was the important part to the majority of the people present. But Vicky Ruvolo wished she had an explanation.

Vicky wept as she watched Ryan crying during his guilty plea. "He's sorry," she whispered to Benny.

The spectators in the gallery pews remained seated as the court officers escorted Ryan and his attorneys out of the courtroom.

When the teen reached the row where Vicky was seated, he stopped. The court officers nervously tried to move him along, but then backed off when they realized the encounter was not going to be hostile.

Keahon put a hand on his client's shoulder. "Say to her whatever it is you feel," he coaxed.

The victim and her attacker suddenly embraced each other, openly crying. Spectators and reporters alike strained to hear what Ryan was saying, as he quietly apologized to Vicky for what he'd done before collapsing into loud sobs. "I'm so thankful and happy that you are doing well," Ryan said to her. The two of them held hands and hugged repeatedly. She caressed his cheek with her palm and rubbed his back.

"You're such a wonderful person," he said, sobbing uncontrollably. "Never did I intend to hurt anyone, especially someone as special as you. I prayed for you every night, I never meant this to happen."

"It's okay, it's okay," she said. "I am going to be watching you now. Just do good with your life."

As Ryan left the courtroom, Vicky turned to Benny. "I needed that hug as much as he did," she confided.

Outside, Ryan addressed the reporters, photographers and TV crews who had been waiting for him. "She is one of the most important people in my life. She had my life in her hands and didn't take advantage of that. She is a wonderful person. I love that woman."

Back inside the courtroom, Suffolk County DA Tom Spota quietly chatted with Vicky. "I believe you really did do the right thing," he said.

"God gave me a second chance at life and I just passed it on," she responded.

What happened in the courtroom that day between Ryan and Vicky made front-page news in local daily newspapers and in evening news shows in the New York region.

Producers from TV outlets across the U.S. soon started calling Vicky, asking her to appear on their shows. In the days that followed, she appeared on NBC's *Today Show* and ABC's *Good Morning America*.

There was an insatiable curiosity about what had enabled Victoria Ruvolo to step forward and advocate on behalf of her assailant. With her civil suit still pending, she had not forgiven Ryan Cushing for what he had done. But, she'd found a way to act mercifully. Her message of kindness resonated with people inside and outside the courtroom.

In that moment, Victoria was less a victim and more a teacher. News of her story inspired hundreds of well-wishers to write cards and letters of praise. The messages came from victims and offenders alike.

There was even a note from then New York State Senator and current Secretary of State Hillary Rodham Clinton commending her for her actions.

Victoria was named as one of the top ten people who influenced 2005 by the Arts and Entertainment Channel. Beliefnet.com, a multi-faith Internet community, voted her the most inspirational person of 2005. Others who were nominated included Bono, Rosa Parks, and David Rozelle, an American soldier who lost his foot in Iraq and returned there to fight again after his recovery.

Beliefnet.com commented, "If Victoria Ruvolo can manage to quell her anger, summon such wisdom, and sense of gratitude in the wake of such a calamity, can't we do the same in less difficult situations?"

CHAPTER THIRTEEN

"Justice has nothing to do with what goes on in a courtroom; Justice is what comes out of a courtroom."

Clarence Darrow

Nearly ten months had passed from when Ryan let go of the turkey until he said "I'm sorry" to Vicky. Words of apology are rarely uttered in the courtroom. When they are said, they usually follow a protracted and contentious litigation, or plea negotiations in which new wounds have been opened.

Research has shown that when doctors apologize to their patients immediately after an unfortunate outcome, the likelihood of a medical malpractice suit decreases. Doctors are human, just like the rest of us. An admission of fallibility makes their humanity accessible to us.

The opposing sides in a trial rarely meet before litigation. In the time period before opening arguments, attorneys advise their clients not to say "I'm sorry" because remorse might be mistaken for an admission of guilt. On the flip side, accepting an apology, such as

Vicky had done when she said "It's okay" might have construed a wrong message to Ryan's lawyers.

Vicky's personal injury attorney, Paul Feur, was concerned that "It's okay" would be perceived by some people that Victoria was somehow okay with what Ryan had done, and therefore he would be relieved of any obligation to make restitution for her pain, suffering, and financial losses. This is the world in which lawyers nitpick in order to protect their clients. But this is really not a way to heal relationships.

In my work with juvenile probationers at Suffolk County's Probation Department, we sometimes attempt to bring a victim and offender together, hoping to mitigate the harm caused by the juvenile and make him aware of the affect his act has had upon the person or the community. But those attempts are often thwarted by lawyers because there is a pending lawsuit or an order of protection that prohibits contact between the parties.

"It felt good to finally confront the person who had caused me such harm," Vicky remarked after their courtroom encounter. "Seeing him before me enabled me to know him in a way that I couldn't have before. Ryan's actions were further proof that my decision to show him leniency had been the right one," Vicky explained. "With his plea bargain already in place, he could have just walked out of the courtroom that day without even acknowledging me. But he didn't."

As Victoria explained to me later, when she held Ryan in her arms, her maternal instinct took over. As she tried to calm his uncontrollable sobs, she felt empathy for him, no matter the pain he had caused her, and she had reached out to comfort him. When Vicky said, "It's okay," she did not mean that she was absolving him from consequences for what he had done. Rather, she meant that she would not allow his action to have power over her, that it was time for them both to move forward.

Vicky didn't mean to suggest that Ryan was not responsible, and therefore should not be held accountable. Rather, she had freed herself from the bonds of anger, fear, and resentment. To clarify any mistaken belief that Victoria was "okay" with what Ryan had done, she labored over a statement that she intended to read at Ryan's sentencing, scheduled for later that month.

Sometimes, forgiveness is perceived as being soft on the perpetrator. But as Vicky would later explain to me, forgiveness is not about letting anyone off the hook or excusing someone else's responsibility in an action, or forgetting the offense. It is about the freedom that follows for the forgiver when resentment, regret and anger are cast off. To Victoria, forgiving Ryan was in her best interest. "I would have still been trying to get out of St. Charles Rehabilitation if I did not let go of any feelings of vengeance," she later told me.

Though untrained in this area and operating solely on her own intuition, Vicky was making the right decision for herself. Indeed, scientific studies affirm that she did the right thing. Stress-induced reactions to violent crime include killer cell cytotoxicity, autoimmune suppression, disruption of personal relationships, Acute Coronary Syndrome, and consequent increased mortality, according to author Robert Grant, Ph.D.

Victoria never needed Ryan to say he was sorry. But the fact that he did reaffirmed her belief that she had done the right thing. The plea was already in place, so Ryan did not have to seek her out to embrace her. Their hug seemed to show the courtroom a Buddhist principal-in–action - that forgiveness does not mean absolution but is an opportunity for the inner transformation of both victim and perpetrator.

Vicky's brother-in-law, Benny, had been her primary caretaker during her long months of recuperation. Perhaps more than anyone else, he had seen her suffer. Witnessing Ryan and Vicky embracing that day had made him decide to revisit his own pain from losing Benny Boy. He'd been carrying the intense emotional drain with him since the accident. Suddenly, he felt compelled to seek out the man who had taken his son's life. Maybe meeting the man would provide the catharsis he desired.

Secretly, he searched out the individual and went to see him without anyone in his family knowing.

The meeting was emotional. Benny learned a lot from the encounter. The man who'd been driving had been grappling with his own pain, shame, and guilt. However, the man was a decent person.

Benny knew that he was taking a risk. There was the possibility that the meeting wouldn't go well, and that he would feel no relief. But he followed Vicky's example and took a chance. He left the meeting with a sense of closure that he'd never had before.

———————

Through forgiveness, reconciliation is attainable. Reconciliation is the restoration of an old relationship or the creation of a new one. Given the sterile nature of the justice system, it rarely happens. Only when the victim and offender seek each other out, as in the case of Victoria and Ryan, is reconciliation a possibility.

In human relationships, when legal bars to communication are absent, forgiveness creates room for empathy for both sides and therefore greater likelihood for reconciliation. I had never witnessed reconciliation in a criminal matter. Perhaps this is what made this case so amazing to me.

Taking Victoria's lead, I decided to go visit my uncle unannounced. When he came to the door, he seemed shocked and surprised. I embraced him, and he joined me in the embrace. It was like nothing had happened between us. The relationship between my uncle and me had always been superficial. My uncle was on his way out with a friend to play golf, but he invited me inside. I showed him videotapes of my children on my iPhone and I got to Face Chat with my cousin and her ten-month-old child.

My Aunt Chris arrived home soon thereafter. She was tearful. She is originally from Belgium and has no local family ties. She met my uncle while he was attending medical school in Belgium. After about 45 minutes, my uncle left with his friend for the golf course. He did not appear upset at all and wished me good health. My Aunt Chris and I were left alone in the kitchen to speak. She told me that I owed her an apology. I was surprised, because I remembered apologizing to her when I had called back to invite her to my mother's funeral. However, she had no recollection of that apology.

I am grateful that I had the opportunity to apologize to her once again and to explain to her that she just happened to be the one who picked up the phone that day. She appeared to understand and have empathy for me as I explained the circumstances, that I was seeing my mother's dead body for the first time and looking for someone to blame. I gave her my number and I hope that she comes to see my children. Ah, the power of dialogue and reconciliation.

I was grateful that my aunt had continued to visit my mother and I got an opportunity to thank her personally. As for my uncle, I have already forgiven him for not visiting my mom. I do not know if we will continue to have a relationship, but I feel at peace. When I left my aunt that afternoon, I told her that I came in honor of my mother. I hope she appreciated it and she too is in less pain.

CHAPTER FOURTEEN

> # "Nothing is easier than to denounce the evildoer, and nothing is more difficult than to understand him."

Fyodor Dostoevsky

I have seen many teens impelled to criminal acts for no other reason than they were bored. I have also learned in my years as a practicing psychologist with an interest in neuroscience that the emotional part of the adolescent brain is responsible for making decisions because the executive region of the brain is not fully developed. This revealing research offers explanations as to why teenagers engage in impulsive and risky behaviors and why it may be difficult to parent a child who looks and often sounds like an adult, yet has a brain that still has not matured.

For many reasons, Victoria's story held my rapt attention. She refused to become discouraged, despite all the tragic things that had happened to her and her family. She refused to give up on Ryan, like so many others in the community had done.

Vicky had no advanced degrees to help her decide what was right and wrong. She had a sense of determination, a willingness to forge ahead no matter how hard the path. She did what she thought was right without being righteous, no matter what others had to say.

While I was impressed with her resilience and spirit, her sense of justice toward Ryan intrigued me the most. I began to ponder what lessons could be learned from this woman's willingness to ask for mercy for the boy whose act of criminal negligence had almost killed her.

From the moment I read Victoria's quote in *The New York Times*, challenging Ryan to make his the life the best it could be, I wanted to create a venue where this could happen.

The summer months had not warmed my heart since my mother's death that past January. I was still angry at the world for taking her away from me, and I could not make sense of it. I did find solace in my work at Suffolk County's Probation Department where I was tasked with helping to prevent juveniles from becoming repeat offenders. I was already using Vicky's story to talk to children and their families about the consequences of making bad choices. That work was based on my studies and the research I had done as a graduate student at Hofstra University prior to being hired by the Probation Department.

I created a program called TASTE, the acronym standing for "Thinking errors," "Anger Management," "Social Skills" and "Talking Empathy." The goal is twofold: to engage the family in a therapeutic intervention that gives the family members a sense of what therapy is with hopes of demystifying the process, and to help prevent thinking errors from recurring. It targets all incoming adolescent youth who have been sentenced to probation supervision, and it runs on a four-week-long cycle continuously throughout the year.

In the first week, we expose the kids to what thinking errors are, such as blaming others for their mistakes. We then retell the story of what happened to Victoria and ask the juvenile participants to discern what type of thinking errors were made before this happened so that

94

they may then discover the thinking errors in their own crime. More than likely the teens in Victoria's case had never thought about Erica Karnes, the owner of the stolen credit card, and whether or not she would get stuck with the bill for their night of revelry. Perhaps they reasoned that once the card was reported stolen, she would not have to pay the bill.Such attempts at rationalization are called "thinking errors."

During one of my classes, I began to wonder if it would be possible to have Ryan come to speak before the participants in my program. Perhaps I could help fulfill Victoria's wish by having Ryan complete his one-year community service through speaking to children and their families in the first week of the TASTE program.

The greatest challenge an individual faces after incarceration is finding reintegration into a society that has defined him by his criminal act. By speaking to children who have been placed on probation, Ryan would be able to find redemption through service and at the same time promote healing for Victoria.

Ryan's upbringing was not unusually harsh. He had the same kind of childhood that many kids have, with moderate amounts of tension and chaos. His parents were divorced. He suffered with albinism, which caused him to stand out from his peers and have trouble with his vision. Kids pick on anyone who is not like them, especially during adolescence when there is hyper-vigilance and sensitivity about appearance, so perhaps Ryan was bullied.

Like any other child, Ryan longed to fit in with the other kids his age. However, the people he chose as friends were prone to mischief and trouble.

As parents, we wish that our children would find the "good kids" to hang out with, hoping that good peers will ensure our children's own good behavior. Many of us preach tolerance and respect and won't tolerate racism or other sorts of bigotry. We disavow bullying. But our best efforts sometimes fall short.

Perhaps the schools Ryan attended didn't take swift enough action to end the bullying. Perhaps the community hadn't provided enough facilities and activities for teens. Maybe there was a lot of blame to go around. But, this wasn't about placing blame; it was about giving one mixed-up teen a second chance to be a productive citizen.

Sending Ryan to jail for twenty years, until he was in his late 30's, would certainly have punished him; but it would most likely also have hardened him and created a man harboring anger and hate.

Vicky spent some time speculating on how a prison term would affect Ryan, but she had seen too many personal tragedies in her own life to dwell on it. Her eldest brother, Billy, never had the opportunity at a second chance. He'd lost his life because of his foolish decision to do drugs. Now, she was confronted with another teen who had made a serious mistake. While she wasn't ready to forgive Ryan for what he'd done, Victoria was ready to show him mercy and give him a second chance.

Vicky did ask the simple question "why?" Our justice system may be good at finding facts, but it has never been good at seeking to understand the underlying reason why a person commits a crime. According to Fyodor Dostoevsky, "Nothing is easier than to denounce the evildoer, and nothing is more difficult than to understand him." In asking "why" we can hope for new understandings. The justice system is bound by time limitations and practicality that constrict its world, allowing it to only delve concretely: black or white, guilt or innocence.

This simplification invades our own personal relationships and guides our navigation through conflict. The tendency to think in terms of right vs. wrong can interfere with the opportunity for a mutual understanding. Once we are locked into our position, the inability to have a dialogue enables and perpetuates the anger.

I had a similar experience in my own life. When I was fourteen, I left my junior high school for another school after someone drew swastikas on my locker. I no longer felt comfortable or welcome in my own school. The kids who were responsible were never caught, but without even knowing who they were, I hated them for what they had done. I swore to myself that if I ever found them, I would beat the crap out of them.

I held onto that grudge for twenty-six years, until I was called upon to conduct a mental health evaluation on a child who had drawn swastikas in the boy's bathroom in the very same junior high school. Sitting before him, I allowed myself to see him for who and what he was, and my rage dissipated. He did not even know the meaning of a swastika. He had both learning and emotional disabilities and came from a troubled past.

Although I never discovered who drew the swastika on my locker, I liberated myself from feelings of anger. When I changed my question from "who?" to "why?" I finally realized that I didn't have to take the action as personal, where anger usually begins.

———————

Victoria's decision to ask "why?" transformed a community. By seeking to understand the outrageousness of throwing a turkey out of a car, Victoria was able to convert a system of justice away from a 'punishment' objective and toward a healing objective. Slowly, Victoria was able to convince the District Attorney that a twenty-five-year sentence would meet neither her nor Ryan's needs.

The movement toward healing was not limited to the D.A. The same media that had demonized Ryan now focused on Victoria and her humanity, calling her act "a moment of grace."

Ryan had done something reckless and wrong. But that did not prevent Victoria from believing he deserved a second chance.

When Victoria asked "why?" she saw Ryan transform before her eyes. Instead of a callous evildoer, she saw a troubled young man from a broken home who was physically handicapped with partial blindness. In no way did that excuse his behavior, but it helped guide and empower her to make her recommendation to the District

Attorney's Office. Her innate compassion led her to reason, "What would be the purpose of ruining this young man's life by sending him away for twenty-five years?"

————————————

Prior to sentencing a defendant, it is the role of the probation department to prepare a pre-sentence investigation for the court. The report contains background information about the defendant as well as victim impact information. I wanted to recommend Ryan's participation in the TASTE program as part of his rehabilitation. But first, I had to get Victoria's permission.

I was initially too nervous to speak to her, so I called the probation officer who was preparing the sentencing report and asked her to run my idea past Vicky: Would Ryan's participation in my TASTE program be acceptable to her as a form of community service? I thought I might also be able to get an audio recording of Victoria discussing the incident and her sense of empathy for others, which could also be used in the program.

I was excited when the probation officer called back and said, "Dr. Goldman, Victoria thinks it would be a great form of community service for Ryan to participate in the program, and she would love to talk to you about her own public speaking."

Speaking to Victoria over the phone was a thrill for me, although it also made me quite nervous. She had attained celebrity status in New York and I was in awe of her handling of the situation with Ryan. While she may not have been a U.S. Supreme Court judge or a famous psychologist, the rock stars of my world, I was honored nonetheless to make that call. Still, I did not know what to expect. Would she speak slowly as a result of her injuries? Would she stutter? Would she not understand?

"Hello, Ms. Ruvolo, I am Dr. Goldman from the Probation Department. Thank you so much for speaking with me," I said cautiously.

"Oh, please call me Vicky," she replied, instantly setting me at ease.

"I think what you did was amazing, I have been talking about your story to the kids here at Probation."

"Oh, I am honored," she said.

"I think it is great that you want Ryan to speak at the TASTE program, what better service than for him to have to come before a bunch of kids and talk about what a stupid, ridiculous thing he did."

As we talked about what she'd gone through, I was taken with her intuition about human nature and the importance of giving an individual the opportunity to repair the harm he had caused. The theory is simple, but it's often missed by the justice system.

Victoria saw her assailants as "a bunch of kids who committed a stupid act." The "group think" wanted severe justice, but Victoria refused to get caught up in that current. When she asked "why?" she took her power back. No longer was she the meek victim of a horrific act, but rather the empowered, compassionate survivor, willing to face her assailants.

When Victoria was able to shed the "victim" role, she took away the power of her assailants and overcame her fear. In the *Wizard of Oz*, when Dorothy sees that the Wizard is only a man, she realizes that the power to choose her path rests with her, not the Wizard. But it is the Wizard who steers her toward this awareness.

Would Vicky be willing to talk to the teens and parents attending my TASTE program sessions? I worried that asking her to repeatedly retell her painful story to a group of strangers would be stressful. To make matters worse, I had no way to pay for speakers for my program. I asked if she'd be willing to have me videotape her, and then allow me to show the tape to my classes.

"What? Are you crazy? Why videotape me, when you can have the real thing?" Vicky responded.

I was stunned, but happily agreed to have her join me.

CHAPTER FIFTEEN

"Crime is a wound, and justice is about healing."

Daniel Van Ness, lawyer & justice advocate

Two months had passed since the infamous embrace between Ryan and Victoria in the courtroom. On October 17, 2005, Victoria and her family arrived at the Riverhead courthouse and assumed their same seats in the second row of the courtroom's gallery. It seemed to Victoria that even more cameras were outside the courtroom than the last time she came to Riverhead. This would be the day that Ryan would be sentenced.

"On the sentence calendar, People versus Ryan Cushing," the court clerk bellowed. Suffolk County Criminal Court in Riverhead was in session. Ryan and his attorneys stepped to the rail.

"Good afternoon, Counsel. Mr. Cushing appears today for sentencing having entered into a plea of guilty to the crime of Assault in the Second Degree," the judge said. "Both sides have been furnished a copy of the pre-sentence investigation report; is that correct?"

Both attorneys answered in the affirmative.

"Ms. Clifford, it's my understanding you have advised the Court that Ms. Ruvolo, the victim in this matter, wishes to address the Court with respect to sentencing," the judge inquired.

"Yes, and I would ask the Court's permission for Victoria Ruvolo to step up to the lectern," Clifford responded.

Vicky noticed that Ryan was not accompanied by anyone. She did not see either of his parents seated near the front of the courtroom. Vicky thought about her own parents, and wondered what kind of individual would leave a son to fend for himself in a court of law. She felt firmer than ever in her resolve to push for a light sentence for Ryan. Perhaps she could show this boy what it meant to have someone care about him.

Vicky rose and walked forward to address the court. Gone were the shuffle in her step that she had struggled to overcome in physical therapy and the wiring in her teeth that had prevented her from speaking for weeks, but had allowed her jaw to heal. Gone, too, was the anger that she'd experienced soon after the incident.

Standing before the court and addressing her remarks at Ryan, Vicky said, "I believe that no matter what we do in life, all things have a consequence. I believe that what you give in life comes back to you. If you do good things, good will come in return. Without hesitation or thought, this is how I have always lived my life. There could be no better example of this than in my standing here speaking today.

"Others have misinterpreted our emotional response, which occurred at our first meeting as an indication that I have forgiven you, which I have not, in the sense that I have not absolved you. I expect you to serve the consequences of your actions, both criminal and civil, but I truly hope that by demonstrating compassion and leniency, I have encouraged you to seek an honorable life. If my generosity will help you mature into a responsible, honest man, whose graciousness is a source of pride to your loved ones and your community, then I will be truly gratified, and my suffering will not have been in vain.

"I leave you with this advice: everything we do and everything we give will eventually come back to us," Vicky said. "I also believe that sometimes different paths cross for one reason or another. Ryan, prove me right."

"Does Mr. Cushing wish to address the Court prior to sentencing?" Judge Kahn asked.

Ryan grabbed his handwritten notes from his inside pocket. His hands began to shake as he held the paper flush with his face. The teen's limited vision meant that he had to hold the paper close in order to read it.

Turning toward Vicky, Ryan began his remarks in a barely audible voice: "Ms. Ruvolo, I want to tell you again how sorry I am for the pain you have suffered. Never did I intend to hurt anyone, especially someone as extraordinary and special as you. I have learned that life is really about the choices you make, especially when faced with trying situations. I was so relieved to finally meet you and see for myself that you were doing well. There wasn't a day that went by I didn't think of you.

"Throughout our lives seldom do we have the chance to connect with the special person who possesses so much love and compassion. Your ability to forgive me has had a profound effect on me. It has already made a positive change in my life. Life is not only about the choices you make, it is about learning from the bad choices you make; it is about learning from those choices and those consequences, good or bad. Ms. Ruvolo, I wish you the best that life has to offer you. You deserve it. Thank you for everything. I'm sorry."

As author and attorney Daniel Van Ness once wrote, "Crime is a wound and justice is about healing." <u>With vengeance there can be no healing.</u>

Victoria walked away from the lectern tearful but resolute that she had found justice. Instead of the lengthy prison sentence, Ryan was ordered to serve six months in the Suffolk County Jail, five years probation and, as a form of community service, he was required to participate for one year in the rehabilitation program for at-risk

RUVOLO, GOLDMAN, PULITZER

juvenile offenders that I had been running for the County's Probation Department.

Victoria noticed two court officers walking over to Ryan and standing behind him. She heard a clicking sound as one of the officers removed handcuffs from his belt. "Put your hands behind your back", he ordered the teen.

She watched the officer snap the cuffs on Ryan's thin wrists and caught his gaze when he looked over again at her and her family. Victoria could not stop herself from welling up with tears as Ryan was escorted out the side entrance.

Judge Kahn addressed Victoria directly, "Ms. Ruvolo, I am thoroughly happy to have had the opportunity to have contact with such an extraordinary person. I wish you the very best."

Victoria's wisdom would hopefully be a model of courage. She defined justice on her own terms. Victoria felt that imposing a twenty-five-year prison term would be counterproductive. She did not want to ruin Ryan's life. She wanted him to take advantage of his second chance in a meaningful way. She had emerged from her brush with death as a more emotionally and spiritually empowered person, free from vindictiveness.

Nevertheless, to this day, she gets upset that not one of the teenagers had showed the decency to come back or call 911. Victoria wouldn't leave an animal to suffer on the side of the road, let alone her fellow man.

Her ordeal has had a profound effect on her, and she has learned to truly appreciate the preciousness of life. Each day when she wakes up, she thanks God simply because she is alive.

By seeking to understand her assailant and the law, Victoria became an educated victim. While she wanted Ryan to understand what losing freedom was like, Victoria also challenged Ryan to make himself a better person in their memorable embrace. While Ryan's attorneys had asked that his record of conviction be sealed, Victoria intuitively responded, "If I have to be reminded by the scar where the tracheotomy tube was, then Ryan's record should not be sealed."

T.J. Parsell, who at the time was writing a memoir about his experiences in prison, wrote an editorial for the New York Times about how a prison sentence presented many dangers for someone like Ryan.

"I see a lot of myself in Ryan Cushing. He's a shy, skinny troubled teenager, who, for whatever reason, was unable to comprehend the possible consequences of his actions. Back in 1978, anyone could have looked at me and predicted that I'd have problems in jail. Today, I'm thinking about Ryan Cushing. I applaud Victoria Ruvolo's ability to forgive, but mostly I hope that her last request is also met - that someday, he'll be able to move on and make his life the best it can be."

CHAPTER SIXTEEN

"Do good with your life."

Victoria Ruvolo

I t was November 29, 2005, one year since Victoria awoke from her medically-induced coma, and she was scheduled to speak to the teens in my TASTE program for the first time. We'd agreed to meet privately first so that we could chat. I was concerned about the project's impact on her time, and I didn't want to schedule another appointment for the two of us to review and rehearse her presentation. We decided that we'd keep things informal and just wing it.

That day, I could not focus on my work at the probation department. I was finally going to get the opportunity to meet the woman whose story I had followed so closely. Although we had spoken by phone and I had seen pictures of her in the newspaper, I did not quite know what to expect.

"Dr. Goldman, your appointment is here," my assistant said.

I could not believe how good Victoria looked. Given all of the injuries that I had read about, I thought she would have some obvious scarring. But that wasn't the case.

I was also taken by how strong she appeared. She did not seem like a victim. Her voice was rich with energy. Despite my attempts to be sensitive to any concerns, Victoria had no fears. She kept saying, "No big deal."

It was 6:00 p.m. and the group of parents and kids were ushered into the conference room. No one appeared to recognize Victoria as they passed her.

I had asked Vicky to speak during the last of the program's four sessions, titled "Talking Empathy." Given the self-centered nature of the teenager, trying to teach empathy to adolescents seems like an insurmountable task. But I had been using Victoria's story in my remarks as an effective example of what it means to truly have empathy. However, I had never had Victoria present to make the story real.

Ryan was still in jail at the time and so had not begun participating in the program. My plan was to have him speak during the first session to discuss what thinking errors he had made that resulted in his crime as part of his one-year community service.

Not knowing that she was in the room, the audience listened as I retold the story of Victoria from her point of view. I stopped at the picture showing her face after the ten hours of reconstructive surgery. I asked a boy, who was sitting next to his mother, what he would do if he came to visit his mother in the hospital in this condition and learned that she had been injured in the same manner as Victoria.

Intuitively, the child replied, "I would find the kids who did it and I would throw something at them."

"The victim becomes the victimizer," I said. "What do you think the victim is thinking?"

Hurling their responses at me, they interjected, "pain, anger, revenge."

When they were finished I told them, "Well, you know what? We don't have to guess because she is right here."

As Vicky stood up, I heard the hushed sounds of "Oh my God, holy shit!"

I knew they would be shocked. Perhaps I was even more shocked as Vicky spoke to the group about all of her personal losses; the death of her 19-year-old brother from an overdose; the death of her 25-year-old brother Tommy in the car crash; the murder of her brother-in-law Jamesy on Brooklyn's Interboro Parkway; and the death of her 15-year-old nephew Benny, killed while riding his bike delivering newspapers. She spoke about losing her baby during the eighth month of her pregnancy, too.

I was moved as Victoria spoke about the details of her painful surgery, and I realized that I was not alone. I saw the teens in the room listening intently and crying. I was in awe at the empathetic transformations I was witnessing.

Despite all of these losses, Victoria explained that she never viewed herself as a victim. Instead, she said she tried to take on many of the good traits of those who had died as a way to continue their legacy.

As Victoria spoke, I realized that by bringing this program together and making it happen, I was honoring my mother. As long as I am doing good deeds in honor of my mother, her legacy is not lost. Victoria was speaking to parents and kids in the audience, but inadvertently she was also speaking to me. Victoria was able to find humor in her sadness, something she said she had learned from her mother. It was an important quality to have in coping with tragedy.

"Well at least they didn't throw a ham at me, because then I would have been known as Miss Piggy," she joked wryly. Victoria was an endearing treasure trove of one-liners.

At the end of the presentation, many of the parents and children cried as they embraced her. They told her that they had prayed for her while she was in the hospital. Graciously, Victoria thanked them and told them that she believed that their prayers were the reason she was still alive.

After the families had left, I thanked Victoria profusely. She told me she had a wonderful time and, to my surprise, thanked me for "making sense of this senseless act." She offered her speaking services to me at any time.

"If I have a chance to help anyone, I will always be there," she said. She has never let me down.

———————

While Ryan ate his Thanksgiving Day turkey in jail, Victoria invited Jo-Marie, Jimmy, Billy and Jillian, to her home to celebrate the holiday. She joked that her only form of vengeance would be cooking a 20-pound turkey for the family. As she bent over to lift the turkey out of the oven, her laughter turned into a prayer of gratitude. Looking up at the ceiling, she said, "Thank you, God. You must really love me!"

It was a miracle that she had lived through the incident and now was able to continue a near-normal life, complete with cooking a holiday turkey for her family.

———————

Vicky's search for meaning behind her suffering was guided by her faith in humanity and love of life. She hoped that some of the compassion that she had shown Ryan would enter his heart and motivate his actions in the community.

On February 9, 2006, approximately four months after the date he was sentenced, Ryan was released from the Suffolk County jail. Leaving jail meant that Ryan would be faced with Vicky's challenge, to do something positive with his life.

After completing his one-year of mandatory service with the TASTE program, Ryan renewed Victoria's faith that she had done the right thing when he volunteered to continue speaking at the TASTE program for another three years. Ryan has inspired other children on probation to participate in the public speaking part of the TASTE program. He has become a role model for this population as many of them have joined his cause and have spoken to other children about the mistakes they have made. Ryan has come a long way toward being a responsible, mature, respected member of the community. He has taken Victoria's advice to heart, and we are all the better for his second chance, made possible by Victoria's wisdom.

EPILOGUE

IT HAS BEEN SIX YEARS since Victoria began speaking at the TASTE program. Her message never gets tired and her energy remains strong and enthusiastic. Along the way, she has impacted and transformed many lives. She has met nurses who cared for her at the hospital. She has received letters from strangers, claiming that she is responsible for their ability to move forward. Others have sought her out just for guidance in their own life. I am proud to have created a venue where Victoria's message has clearly resonated.

After learning of Erica Karnes's feelings of guilt, Victoria called her to say it wasn't her fault. "You were a victim, too," Victoria told her. The words provided great comfort to Erica, who now works as a dedicated 911 operator, more empathetic than most because of her experience.

Victoria is remembered less for what happened to her than for how she responded to her assailant. In that respect, she has transcended her tragedy. She has given meaning to her suffering. It is clear there is no room for vengeance in Victoria Ruvolo's life.

Her message transcends religious barriers. Chris Williams, a Mormon, has given credit to Victoria Ruvolo for providing him the inspiration to forgive the drunken teenage driver who stuck and killed his wife and two children. After learning about Victoria's story, Williams personally reached out to her to thank her for providing him the inspiration to move on.

Rabbi Jonathon Lubiner of the Jacksonville Jewish Center in Jacksonville, Florida, discussed the TASTE program in a sermon he gave at Yom Kippur. "To pardon means to let go of the hurt; it is a gesture of spirit, not a calculation of payments made. To forgive doesn't ask us to forget about justice, though it does require we forego vengeance."

Victoria's message is clear: for healing and justice to occur, there can be no vengeance. Her message has helped me, as well as countless others, to cope with their losses and has guided some within the legal system to seek justice without vengeance.

Her work with me in the TASTE program has touched and changed many lives and has helped others find meaning from their suffering. Since its inception, more than 5,000 people have completed the TASTE program. The program is now becoming a model for use in other communities across the U.S., both in schools and probationary programs.

On April 14, 2009, the *New York Law Journal*, a weekly publication with a target audience of attorneys and others interested in the law, ran a story about the TASTE program and Ryan and Victoria's participation. The story prompted readers to send me numerous cards and letters.

Many prisoners across the state read the *New York Law Journal* as they contemplate their own cases and appeals. So, it is not a complete surprise when I receive letters from prisoners stating that they wished they had been given an opportunity to repay the community for the harm they had caused. Some also want an opportunity to speak to teens about their own mistakes, hoping that others might learn from their errors. Alas, there is no easy way for me to make that happen.

I am currently working with school officials to bring elements of the TASTE program into more than fifty school districts on Long Island, as part of a broader initiative to lessen the incidents of bullying.

It was Vicky Ruvolo who created the foundation for this work with her simple question "why?" The question is asked far too infrequently in the nation's criminal justice system. We focus on "who did it?" and "what is the appropriate punishment for the individuals involved?" But when we ask the "why," we are more likely to find the means for preventing it from happening again. We find the road to healing.

Granted, the State has standards and goals, which provide a strict

111

timeline within which cases must be disposed of. And so, our system becomes quite concrete, needing a suspect and an arrest, and then defining the individual solely by the criminal act that he or she has committed.

But seeking to understand the person who wronged you generates the possibility for personal healing. It allows you the limitless opportunity to move forward.

This is Victoria Ruvolo's lesson and legacy, one that through both her attitude toward Ryan and her ongoing work continues, both directly and indirectly, to touch and teach, to impact the world.

APPENDIX

Poems by Victoria Ruvolo

To Benny, December 5, 1983:

Lying there so young and helpless
Waiting for a sign,
Wind was blowing down the trees
As tears cried from the sky.
All were trying desperately
To hold on to you so tight,
When I knew in reality
You were already on your flight.
Morning came with sun shining oh so bright
Leaving only memories of you insight.
Though knowing I will never see you is tearing me apart,
I find some comfort knowing you'll always be in my heart.

To Jamesy, A Love Never Known, December 10, 1983:

I would see you come to be
With another someone else, not me.
Into her arms you would go,
Bout my love you could never know.
The yearning that I had inside
To have you near me by my side,
A love so pure, a love so true
A love that you never knew.

To Jamesy, December 10, 1983:

In my heart there lies a love,
A love so warm and true,
That no one could ever take,
I keep it just for you.
Now we are so far apart,
But I know deep inside my heart,
That someday you will come for me
And we will share this love eternally

Others:

To Hope

I wonder what life would be
If we didn't have our precious dreams,
Dreams that give us strength to carry on
Even when everything else is gone.
And when another day is through,
We still have our dreams to hold on to.

To Sadness

Years go by still nothing's changed,
Pains still flows through my veins,
My body aches from loneliness
Yet I still cannot forget,
And when I try to love again,
Pain just waltzes right on in
Filling my heart with memories
Of all the tragedies I have seen
Till I burst with screams of hate,
Why was I dealt this hand from fate?

ROBERT GOLDMAN, J.D., PSY.D. has dedicated himself to working with at-risk youth, particularly those in the juvenile justice system where his program designed to help kids be more aware of the impact of their decisions is an ongoing success. A husband and father, he lives and works in Suffolk County, New York.

ACKNOWLEDGEMENTS

First and foremost, I thank my loving, supportive, and patient wife, Katina Goldman, who has taught me that there is good in all even though some are more flawed than others. I would also like to thank Katina for giving me the two most amazing sons, Danny and Zachary, who center me daily and teach me the importance of living in the moment.

Thanks to my brothers, Steven and David, for their unwavering support and love for me. And my father, Mitchell Goldman, who has taught me the importance of being a "mensch" and treating all people with respect and compassion.

I would also like to thank my friends Mickey Bradley and Amanda Landes for their guidance and support in this endeavor.

To the women and men of the Suffolk County Department of Probation who, under the guidance of their director, John K. Desmond, have demonstrated the true meaning of rehabilitation, I extend my gratitude.

I would also like to acknowledge Suffolk County District Attorney Thomas Spota and Suffolk County Police Commissioner Richard Dormer for their time and access to the amazing people in their respective departments, specifically Nancy Clifford, Pete Mayer, and James Brierton. Thank you Nancy, Peter and James for taking time to meet with me and answering my questions.

To Farmingville volunteer firefighter Jerry Curtin, I extend my heartfelt thanks for taking the time to speak with me and for all that you do as a volunteer.

I would especially like to thank Doctors Prajoy Kadekade, Maisie L. Shindo, Mark Shapiro, Jennifer Semel-Concepcion, and Deborah Smith of Stony Brook Hospital and St. Charles Rehabilitation Center, who took time out of their busy schedules to sit down with me and share their amazing stories.

Thanks to the late Mark Seidler, the late Denny Maloney, Mark Umbreit, Kay Pranis, Gregg Wills, Ronnie and Twila Earle, who have taught me the true power of dialogue. Thank you to Barbara Keller and Carole McNally for creating the opportunity for meeting these amazing people.

I would like to thank Dr. Janice McClean for being the best baby sitter anyone could ask for and her late husband Jack Thornborough for his guidance and support.

And thank you to my mentor and forever teacher, Dr. Paul Meller.

Thank you, Jeff Levy for all of your support.

I would also like to acknowledge Erica Karnes for sharing her story.

To my editorial team, I would like to thank Lisa Pulitzer for her amazing writing and kindness, Douglas Love for his patience and wisdom, Antoinette Kuritz for showing me the way to make this happen, Martha Smith for her insightful editing, and to Maura Teitelbaum for believing in me.

I would also like to thank my cousin Michael Lane for dedicating his time to reading many versions of this story, as did Corinne Malloy, Edward Goldsmith, Laura Harsch, Talia Goldman, Shea Alvarez, Sue Leftcourt, Ilise Reichelscheimer, and Elaine O'Connor, Ross and Barbara Pirtle.

Thank you, Phyllis Pinard, N.P.P. for helping me run the TASTE program all these years. You have never missed a day. Thank you to Probation Officers Viscardi and Panicola for their unwavering assistance in the administration of the TASTE program.

I would like to acknowledge Ryan Cushing for having the courage to volunteer his time to help children learn from their mistakes and inspire them to give back.

I am forever grateful to Victoria Ruvolo, who continues to inspire me on a daily basis.

I am forever grateful to my mother's support system Leta Albritton, Filomena Muggio and Tobi Essrog.

And to my mother, Carole Goldman, who taught me to always have a sweet heart. Mom, I miss you every day.

VICTORIA RUVOLO

is a woman who draws strength from family. Having survived and recovered from an attack that doctors believed would leave her permanently impaired, Victoria has dedicated herself to making young people aware of the consequences of their decisions. Doing so in concert with Robert Goldman, J.D., Psy.D., she has reached over 5000 at-risk adolescents since her injury.

ACKNOWLEDGEMENTS

God – For allowing me to come back so well.

To my Mom and Dad for making me who I am and showing me how to handle life.

To all my family that has passed on – For being in that car with me that night; I felt your presence.

To Louis Erali – for assisting in saving my life.

To all the amazing volunteers at the Farmingville Fire Department who saved my life.

To everyone who thought and prayed for me – I truly believe that is why I am still here.

To Dr. Mark Shapiro, Dr. Maisie L. Shindo and all the staff at Stony Brook University Hospital for their amazing care, especially to Dr. Prajoy Kadekade who made me look the same as I always did, what an amazing job, no one ever knows!

To all of the staff at Saint Charles Rehabilitation Center, especially Marilyn Fabricante, for helping me come back to who I am and helping me get back on my feet.

To the doctors at the Saint Charles Rehabilitation: Jennifer Semel-Concepcion, M.D. and, Deborah Smith, Ph.D.

To Oceanside Outpatient Rehabilitation – Thank you for your wonderful care.

To my wonderful sisters Rita Dierna and Jo-Marie Brennan for always being there for me, and taking care of me the way Mom would have!

To my dear "brothers"- in-law Benny Dierna and James Brennan for always treating me like your younger sister and being by my side when I needed both of you the most.

To Jillian Brennan for having the most beautiful voice and always including me.

To Billy Cesare, your presence and emotional support in my time of need was like being in the presence of your father once again.

To Francine, Jeff, Brianna and Julianna Greenberg for making that beautiful sign and letting me know how much I mean to you.

To Billi Jo Ruvolo & Tina Rivera – For always making me feel like your number one Aunt

To my brother Joey and my sister-in-law Tanya for not letting me out of your thoughts and prayers.

To my nieces and their families in Florida – Terina Dobbins, Dorothy Rose Ruvolo – I always feel your love.

To my dear, dear friends Ray Caputo & David Moore for always making me feel like family and taking care of all my little pets when I could not. I love you guys!

To Ron Ciaccia for being by my side even though I had no idea and taking care of Gucci.

To Dr. Robert Goldman for making this senseless act into something to help others and for being a wonderful kind-hearted man, he and his beautiful family Katina, Danny & Zachary, have become my closest friends.

To Jean Genes for always being such a helpful caring friend and her beautiful children Michael, Patricia, Sara & Matthew for treating me like an aunt.

To Lance Geller for believing in my story and making it come true.

To Lorraine Chaudhry for holding healing circles for me! And keeping me in your thoughts and prayers!

To my work family for always wishing me only the best.

To Extreme Fitness for aiding me in getting in the best shape of my life.

To Wantagh Mazda for putting me a safe reliable SUV Mazda Tribute.

To Thomas Spota, Pete Mayer, Nancy Clifford for having faith in my decision and allowing it to be.

To attorney Paul Feur for allowing me to be true to who I am and always being by my side.

To Detectives James Brierton and Walter Clark, thank you for your perseverance and helping justice to be served.

To Dr. Michael Creta, thank you for keeping me healthy.

To Dr. Robert Berney, thank you for keeping my back straight.

To Alison Oickle for becoming one of my friends and for being so friendly and helpful.

To Josephine, Santi and Renee Giocolano for keeping me in your thoughts and prayers and for being part of the family.

To my dear friends from The Beach House - Linda Schroeder, Cathy Kabot, Betty Whatley, Nancy Thanks for helping to make the summer of 2005 special.

To my dear closest friends: Terry & Doug Tyers, Steve & Cathy DiMartino, Linda &Vinny Klemmer, John & Linda DiMartino, Diane, Dominick & Marisa Anziano, David & Natalie Carcano, Marc & Tracy Pierson, Kristen Eyester, Barbara,& Joe Vincenti, Louis DeLeo, GiGi Bordies, Mary & Ed Krupski, Iris Wolpow for making my life's memories filled with love, joy & lots of laughter. Who could forget Maroon 5 and Adam Levine!

To the churches I have spoken at: United Methodist Church in Smithtown, TruNorth, Church at the Movies - Thank you for filling my heart with warmth and joy and giving me such a wonderful opportunity to meet so many wonderful people.

To Sunshine Prevention Center for Youth & Families, Dr. Carol Carter and the whole staff, thank you for giving me the opportunity to speak, you are really doing wonderful work there and helping so many.

To my neighbors Heidi and Helmet Hos, John and Kelly Hendrickson, Carolyn, Manny and Cathy Vieira, and John and Maureen Dalton, thank you for watching and taking care of my house in my time of need.

To Sachem Animal Hospital, Dr. Barry Lissman, Dr. Harry Camay, Dr.Joseph Palmeri, Dr. John Corso and the entire staff, thank you so much for taking such wonderful care of all my beloved pets.

To Linda Ruvolo Aymar, Larry Ruvolo, Dennis Ruvolo, Dana Ruvolo, Rusty Ruvolo, you see good things do come from bad things; I was able to reconnect with my dear cousins.

To Marc and Annette Kalikow, I will never forget camping that summer with Rita, Benny, Francine & Benny Jr. All I have to say is pantyhose!

In Memory of my dear friend Vinny Friscia, I will always remember our younger days together. They were the best!

LISA PULITZER, a former correspondent for The New York Times, is the author of more than a dozen nonfiction books in the areas of True Crime and Current Events. Among the books she has written are *Stolen Innocence: My Story of Growing up in a Polygamous Sect, Becoming a Teenage Bride, and Breaking Free of Warren Jeffs,* and *Daughters of Juarez: The True Story of Serial Murder South of the Border,* written with Univision's Teresa Rodriguez. Her latest book, *Portrait of a Monster: Joran van der Sloot, A Murder in Peru, and the Natlee Holloway Mystery,* will be released July 5, 2011.